ABOVE AND BEYOND

LEADING AND MANAGING ORGANIZATIONAL CHANGE

DENNIS L. RICHARDSON

authorHOUSE®

AuthorHouse™
1663 Liberty Drive
Bloomington, IN 47403
www.authorhouse.com
Phone: 1 (800) 839-8640

Published by AuthorHouse: 05/05/2017

ISBN: 978-1-5246-9009-0 (sc)
ISBN: 978-1-5246-9007-6 (hc)
ISBN: 978-1-5246-9008-3 (e)

Library of Congress Control Number: 2017905924

Print information available on the last page.

Praise for
Above and Beyond

"Dennis Richardson is the kind of indomitable leader who sees the vision, seizes the opportunity and develops the people. His passionate leadership and management practices are invaluable to leaders guiding their organizations through organizational change."
-EUREKA F. COLLINS
Award-winning author of *Strong Winds Change Lives*

"Lieutenant Commander Richardson is a savvy leader and strategic thinker. *Above and Beyond* explores the fundamental, enduring truths of organizational leadership that hold constant regardless of context or circumstance."
-CLAUDE "HENDU" HENDERSON, JR.
Command Master Chief, USN

"Dennis Richardson has provided one of the best books on leadership and management you'll find. The 'Above and Beyond' principles translate to any level of human interaction in the workplace. I strongly recommend *Above and Beyond* to managers at all levels and academics that teach Leadership, Management, and Organizational Behavior."
-DERRICK JORDAN,
Senior Financial Analyst, WellStar Corporate

DEDICATION

To my supportive and loving wife of 18 years, Shannan L Richardson, who brings out the best of which I am most capable. Together, we have established a simple but sustaining way of life centered on family first. And even through the test of life, you have always been supportive and constant in my growth as a husband, father, son and brother. I love you dearly—OTSS!

To my most treasured possession, my children Daz'sha, Cheyanne, son Trey'ce (BFF) and grandson Daijon. Your blind trust has kept me motivated and inspired on the darkest of days. I love you with the intensity equal to gasping for my last breath!

Lastly, I wholeheartedly dedicate this book to those who inspired it and regrettably will not even read it.

"He who says it cannot be done should get out
of the way of the person doing it"

~ Old Chinese Proverb

CONTENTS

PREFACE

In learning the basic fundamentals of leadership, you may have learned to be assertive and persistent, regardless of challenges, to accomplish the task. But leaders must also buoy the energy and enthusiasm of the people as they oversee the crucial details of process and end product. True leaders never get distracted by minor details, which might jeopardize the desired end state. Above and beyond leaders always triumph, ultimately establishing a sustainable and fruitful organizational model.

In contrast, leaders who tend to focus on the tree rather than studying the entire forest never understand how and why the trees are set in the woodland. Simply stated, those who are incapable of looking beyond the immediate obstacle will typically not advance past their self-imposed limitations. To achieve your highest levels of success, win from within first—then project your leadership vision outward.

In *Above and Beyond*, I share my story of taking ownership of an undesirable situation. I had to make unpopular decisions, yet I ensured success for the organization, making every effort worth my while. Truly, it was easier to succeed than to fail because I didn't delay when faced with the need for cultural change. I strongly believe the first step in getting where you eventually want to be is deciding you are not going to stay where you are. I demonstrated the courage to stick with it, and I ignored the negative energy of unprincipled naysayers. Courage is born within all, but leaders cultivate and nurture it today, tomorrow, and every day thereafter.

I am convinced you cannot fail if you possess the internal fortitude to stick with your assigned task until the end. This dedication is undoubtedly the beginning and ending of success. Anyone can begin, but not all remain steadfast to close the proverbial loop. Maybe yesterday you failed, but today you can succeed—if you stick with it. The great successes of businesses, organizations, and life are repetitions of the same story; it's the story of leaders who did not give up because of difficulties and setbacks. You may not like your current situation, but you most definitely can change most (if not all) its aspects. I know because it happened for me. Today, get ready to lead your organization above and beyond expectations.

ACKNOWLEDGEMENTS

I would like to extend my sincere thanks to all those who supported and encouraged me to write and publish this leadership book, specifically Gregory Collins for imparting his knowledge and expertise throughout this endeavor.

Secondly, I humbly share this publication with the sailors of Assault Craft Unit FOUR (ACU 4), whom I have had the distinct pleasure to serve through this extraordinary journey. I am deeply indebted to both of my previous Commanding and Executive Officers for accepting "Truth to Power" and affording me the opportunity to affect change amidst strong opposition. Thus, I learned to refuse to accept the status quo or succumb to the typical resistance of organizational change.

Thank you to my former fellow Department Heads, affectionately known as the "Fab Five": Tara Jackson, John O'Brien, Matthew Sweet, Matthew Moore, and Tara Snead. Nothing but good times!

I extend my heartiest gratitude to those genuine Chief Petty Officers of Assault Craft Unit FOUR for continuing to demonstrate that aggressive, positive, and focused leadership can solve any number of organizational problems, from substandard practices and poor processes to measurable mission readiness. Chief Petty Officers, when unified—more than any other internal organizational entity—can set the tone for the command and effectively shape naval service. Thank you for your support and continued effort.

Lastly, special thank you to the US Naval Institute for the article "Damn Exec," reprinted with permission; Copyright© (1965) US Naval Institute.

Cover photograph courtesy of Michael MacDonald Photography, LLC.

DISCLAIMERS

The information or material contained in this book, including advice and opinions, are the author's own and do not reflect endorsement by or the views of Assault Craft Unit FOUR, the Department of Defense, the United States Government, or the United States Department of the Navy. The author is solely responsible and liable with respect to the content of this book. Although the words "he," "him," and "his" are used sparingly in this book to enhance communication, they are not intended to be gender driven nor to be an affront to or discriminate against anyone reading this text.

Several unabridged and abridged public domain texts listed on the bibliography page have been adapted, modified, revised and edited to effectively convey exact principles, concepts, or applications—the author makes no claim of ownership—only compilation and editing.

CHAPTER 1

TAKE RESPONSIBILITY

I was serving onboard the USS San Antonio (LPD 17), the lead ship of her class of amphibious transport dock ships, when I received transfer orders from my new command:

> Welcome Aboard and congratulations on your assignment to Assault Craft Unit FOUR, where the Navy's newest and most advanced amphibious assault craft are located. You are about to embark on one of the most challenging and rewarding tours in your naval career. Designed to operate from every well deck configured amphibious ship, the Landing Craft Air Cushion's (LCAC) main mission is to deliver a 60-ton payload to a designated beachhead at speeds in excess of 35 knots. Combining high speed, exceptional maneuverability, and long-range qualities with the ability to travel over land, the LCAC provides added versatility to our Amphibious Forces . . . Welcome Aboard.

After researching the command's history on the Internet, I learned that the LCAC employs air-cushion vehicle technology, combined with state-of-the-art marine gas turbine propulsion. The craft flies on a cushion of air contained within a flexible skirt of synthetic rubberized nylon. This design allows the LCAC to conduct high-speed, over-the-horizon, ship-to-shore movement of Marine Corps assets from amphibious ships to over 70 percent of the world's beaches, compared to only 17 percent using conventional landing craft. In an overload condition, it is capable of carrying a Marine M1A1 Main Battle Tank. It can operate over marshes, reefs, and other areas inaccessible to conventional landing craft. I thought,

WOW! I am going to be the maintenance department head and senior engineer of ACU 4's Fleet Maintenance Activity.

In my excitement, I reviewed the ACU 4 website to find its mission: "To provide combat ready craft that fully meets operational tasking worldwide, on time, every time." I knew then that I was about to be challenged like never before.

I had seen the LCAC while embarked in San Antonio's well deck. With two fully loaded LCAC, the ship was able to transport and land marines with their equipment and supplies from its well deck. The embarked LCAC supported amphibious assault, special operations, or expeditionary warfare missions and served as secondary aviation platforms for amphibious-ready groups. The ability of San Antonio to carry LCAC helped sea warriors execute expeditionary missions throughout the world; this was amazing to watch as I performed my duties as debark control officer and ballast control officer.

I had heard some wonderful things about ACU 4 and was eager to get started. I was highly honored and very proud of the prospect of leading the men and women of MD-FMA at ACU 4. When I arrived in July 2014, I checked in with the executive and commanding officers (XO, CO). I was informed of how, on a daily basis, the sailors demonstrated their commitment to excellence and willingness to go the extra mile to produce first-rate, quality repairs. They stated how the organization had done an extraordinary job of overcoming any and all obstacles by coming up with smart and efficient ways to maintain craft readiness. It was pleasing to hear how the fleet maintenance activity team promoted pride and professionalism at every turn and didn't let declining resources, under-funding, or manpower shortages get in their way. I felt very fortunate to have such a key role in complementing the successes of ACU 4 maintenance.

There was one thing that really stood out about ACU 4, of which I had not taken much notice before. It was their motto: "Above and

Beyond." For me, this slightly redundant expression meant they were exceeding what a particular job required and were exceeding expectations. So, not only was I on the brink of the most challenging and rewarding tour in my naval career, but I had to do more and perform better than would usually be expected of a surface engineer, limited duty officer.

I met with the officer of the fleet maintenance activity and proceeded with the turnover. As the new leader and manager in engineering, maintenance, and repair, I had to own what had been handed to me. It was now on me to lead the only fleet maintenance activity for thirty-five East Coast-based LCAC—valued at twenty-three million dollars each—that provided organizational, intermediate, and depot-level maintenance and repair in support of amphibious striking force capability for Commander, US Fleet Forces Command; Commander, Naval Surface Force, Atlantic; Commander, Expeditionary Strike Group TWO; and Commander, Naval Beach Group TWO.

I had already started instituting a number of minor changes at the MD-FMA, including rebranding the nine shop and work-center areas, capturing and showcasing photographs of the sailors hard at work and getting rid of what I considered clutter in and around the organization. The clutter hampered functionality and threatened future expansion of the command's maintenance and administrative footprint. What appeared to be a major problem, but not a concern to most, was the fundamentals of quality maintenance and repair evidenced by the 37 percent average LCAC readiness (thirteen of thirty-five available for task).

Alarmed at the low LCAC readiness during the weekly status briefings to the commanding officer, I thought, *How can we continue to meet our mission to continuously provide combat-ready craft that fully meet operational tasking worldwide if this number stays low?*

I have to admit, I was quite embarrassed to be briefing the commanding officer of such low LCAC readiness when it was within my scope of responsibility and expertise. I had to do something. First, I established an LCAC status for my MD-FMA team a day prior to briefing the CO. By doing so, I was able ensure the CO received the most accurate information being reported. I will elaborate more in chapter 6. Then, I conducted a ninety-day review of ACU 4's fleet maintenance activity with the LCAC community mid-level managers that revealed a floundering maintenance strategy. Honestly, what we found was a badly broken business model in need of change. In particular, six key areas required our immediate attention:

- Insufficient LCAC crew staffing
- Decreased experienced/skilled personnel
- Broken processes
- Lack of procedural compliance
- Duplication of efforts across the organization
- Challenging cultural habits

To validate our findings, we solicited the help of the aviation community, who conducted a top-down review of our operational and maintenance philosophy. This assessment would prove pivotal later in the development of an executable plan to reshape our maintenance infrastructure. A post-command aviator and maintenance officer conducted a comprehensive review over a two-week period and concluded that ACU 4's LCAC readiness, preventive/corrective maintenance strategy, and repair accomplishment required immediate corrective action. The written report was staggering and indicated our reduction in readiness was due to the issues listed above.

Sufficient LCAC crew members were not available to fully man all LCAC, and a rapid decrease occurred in the number of experienced/ skilled journeyman-level technicians. I was losing institutional knowledge as these technicians were being permanently transferred. This contributed to the decline in overall LCAC readiness.

In addition, managers and supervisors had not trained the sailors in the value of personal ownership and quality maintenance of work. Minimal effort was expended to resolve an issue. If even the most minor hurdles were encountered, sailors and managers were quick to elude a problem with no concern. These attitudes resulted in a *replace* rather than attempt *repair* culture.

To remedy this, all LCAC would be issued to crew members for specific missions, and all personnel, who had not already been assigned to a deploying detachment, would be assigned to shops. Additionally, we would use an aviation model, called Maintenance Control, to become our central location for planning all preventive and corrective maintenance.

The broken processes would be mended with small working groups, reviewing current processes and developing new and improved ones. We thought a two-shift concept, with both night and day shifts staffed as close to 50 percent as possible, including management, would increase LCAC readiness. Both shifts had to have the same fix, form, and function in order to operate effectively. The second shift could not be expected to accomplish their work efficiently without full support. If possible, all command functions had to occur during the overlap period between shifts or be altogether duplicated.

My role as the MD-FMA officer seemed to contradict the efforts of the operations maintenance officer. To streamline efforts, these positions needed to be brought together as maintenance officer and assistant maintenance officer. Our plan would nearly triple the size of the MD-FMA, from 125 up to 370 personnel. Also, I needed to improve the LCAC hourly package tracking through the WEB log database, without operating the LCAC over the required hours (100-, 200-, 300-, 400-, and 500-hour packages). We had to reduce the number of waivers on behalf of the LCAC crew not meeting their proficiency hours.

There was a major lack in procedural compliance. Some reverted to an ambiguous Safe Engineering and Operations Program (SEAOPS) manual standard as opposed to the more appropriate Joint Fleet Maintenance Manual (JFMM). The lack of procedural compliance meant we were not demanding written procedures every time an evolution was performed, to ensure it was followed precisely, in order. No one was checking to ensure the equipment operated as designed.

It is never acceptable to deviate from a written procedure without approval from the commanding officer. However, when a procedure or a result was suspect, some technicians didn't stop to check it. If a procedure is found deficient, procedure dictates it must be formally corrected for future use. Following the prescribed method would reduce wasteful spending in replacing lost tools. We saw the need to rejuvenate two-standard compliance efforts: the fledgling centralized tool issue and accountability program; and direct oversight from supervisors and managers over written procedures. Written procedures included all equipment operating procedures, technical manuals, temporary standing orders, standing orders, standard operating procedures, check lists, emergency procedures, planned maintenance system (PMS) cards, and several others.

In order to prevent duplication of efforts across the organization, we needed effective communication regarding maintenance and repair status during the turnovers from day to night shift. The day shift would review the night shift's completions and plan priorities for the day accordingly. All personnel needed to communicate all information in a very specific way, every time, so that miscommunication would not jeopardize our maintenance efforts.

Therefore, we created pass-down logs to document communication. This confirmation of understanding is critical prior to any change in LCAC or system operation. Since leadership is about getting other people to do what you want them to do, it follows that communication—transmitting information so that it's clearly understood—is vital.

There were plausible existing standards, but the existing culture made them a challenge to enforce. The culture consisted of taking four-day weekends and finding any excuse not to be working (i.e., fun runs, volunteer opportunities, etc.), which produced the perception that outside activities were more important than LCAC readiness. This was the attitude at all levels of the chain of command. The sailors observed leadership taking advantage of the system as it existed and mimicked these behaviors. Additionally, when extended hours were required, sailors at all levels exhibited defiant behavior, and production slowed.

I saw the changes required. I needed to eliminate official half days. If managers thought necessary, we needed to delegate a shop supervisor to handle and stagger assignments throughout the week. I had entered a culture where several managers didn't respect the orders of the department head or division officers without being told the order came from the executive officer. They would not take ownership or accept the assignment. I would give an order, and some would ask me where it came from—this was a red flag. Such skepticism and disrespect had to stop immediately.

As a top-level manager, I give orders that have originated at a higher level of command. Many times, I am simply passing the orders along. One of my managers used the following manner to give his sailors such orders: "LCDR Richardson says we have to be at work on time every morning—no more half-day Fridays." This method of giving orders is common but wrong. When *he* gave this order, he should have stated it as *his* order. What do I mean by this? Here is an example: "Beginning tomorrow, everyone must be at work on time every morning." In this manner, he builds his own authority with subordinates.

But why does it matter? One day the need may arise for him to take charge in an emergency or in absence of superiors. Passing orders in the proper manner preconditions his workers to respond to his commands. The following story, "Damn Exec," by then-Lieutenant Commander Stuart D. Landersman, former executive officer, USS STICKELL (DD 888), should clarify this point:

> The Norfolk wind was streaking the water of Hampton Roads as Commander Martin K. Speaks, U.S. Navy, Commanding Officer of the USS BOWENS (DD 891), stepped from his car, slammed the door, and straightened his cap. As he approached the pier head a sentry stepped from the sentry hut and saluted.
>
> "Good morning, Captain."
>
> "Good morning, Kowalski," answered Commander Speaks. He took pleasure in the fact that he knew the sailor's name. Kowalski was a good sailor. He had served his entire first cruise in the BOWENS and did his work well.
>
> The Captain noticed that over his blues Kowalski wore a deck force foul weather jacket, faded, frayed, dirty, and spotted with red lead. "Little chilly this morning," said the Captain as he walked by. "Yes sir, sure is," replied the sailor with his usual grin.
>
> As the Captain approached his quarterdeck there was the usual scurrying of people and four gongs sounded. "BOWENS arriving," spoke the loudspeaker system, and Lieutenant (j.g.) Henry Graven, U.S. Naval Reserve, gunnery officer and the day's command duty officer, came running to the quarterdeck. Salutes

and cheerful "good mornings" were exchanged, and the Captain continued to his cabin.

Lieutenant Graven looked over the quarterdeck and frowned. "Let's get this brightwork polished chief."

"It's already been done once this morning, sir," replied the OOD.

"Well, better do it again. The Exec will have a fit if he sees it this way," said Graven, again on the quarterdeck."

Later that morning Captain Speaks was going over some charts with the ship's Executive Officer, Lieutenant Commander Steven A. Lassiter, U.S. Navy. The Captain had just finished his coffee and lighted a cigarette. "Steve, I noticed our pier sentry in an odd outfit this morning. He had a foul weather jacket on over his blues; it looked pretty bad."

"Yes sir. Well, it gets cold out there, and these deck force boys have mighty bad looking jackets," the Exec said.

The Captain felt the Exec had missed his point and said, "Oh, I realize they have to wear a jacket, but for a military watch like that, I'd like to see them wear pea coats when it's cold."

Lieutenant Graven was talking with a third class boatswain's mate on the fantail when the quarterdeck messenger found him. When told that the Executive Officer wanted to see him, Graven ended his discussion with, "There, hear that? He probably wants to see me about that brightwork. I don't care how many men it takes to do it, the Exec told me to be sure to get that brightwork polished every morning."

The Executive Officer indicated a chair to Graven and they both lighted up cigarettes. "How's it going these days?" asked the Exec.

Lassiter had always liked Graven, but in the past few months, since he had taken over as senior watch officer, Graven seemed to have more problems than usual.

"Okay, I guess," Graven replied with a forced grin. He knew things were not as they used to be. It seemed strange, too, because everyone on the ship had been so glad to be rid of the previous senior watch officer, that "damn" Lieutenant Dumphy. The junior officers even had a special little beer bust at the club to celebrate Dumphy's leaving and Craven's "fleeting up" to senior watch officer. Now the Exec was always after him. The junior officers didn't help much either, always complaining about the Exec. Maybe the Exec was taking over as "the heel" now that Dumphy was gone.

"That's good," said the Exec, "here's a little thing that you might look into. These men that stand pier watches have to wear a jacket, but the foul weather jacket doesn't look good for a military watch. I'd like to see them wear their pea coats when it's cold." Graven had expected something like this, more of the Exec's picking on him. He responded properly, got up, and left.

Graven told his First Lieutenant: "The Exec says the pier head sentries can't wear foul weather jackets anymore. If it's cold they can wear pea coats," he added.

"But the pea coats will get dirty and then what about personnel inspections?" asked the First Lieutenant.

"I don't know," Graven shook his head, "but if the Exec wants pea coats, we give him pea coats!"

"Pea coats!" said the chief boatswain's mate, "Who says so?"

"That's what the Exec wants," said the First Lieutenant, "so let's give him pea coats."

"The Exec says pea coats for the pier sentries when it's cold," announced the Chief to his boatswain's mates.

A third class boatswain's mate walked away from the group with a buddy, turned and said, "That Damn Exec, first I got to have all my men polish brightwork on the quarterdeck, now they got to wear pea coats on sentry duty 'stead of foul weather jackets!"

Seaman Kowalski's relief showed up at the sentry booth at 1150. "Roast beef today," constituted the relieving ceremony.

"Good, I like roast beef," was the reply. "Hey, how come the pea coat?"

"Damn Exec's idea," said the relief. "We can't wear foul weather gear no more out here, only pea coats."

"Damn Exec," agreed Kowalski, "Captain didn't say nothin' when he came by."

"The Captain's okay, it's just that Damn Exec. He's the guy who fouls up everything," complained the new sentry.

Seaman Kowalski had just gone aboard the ship when Captain Speaks stepped out on the deck to look over his ship. The quarterdeck awning shielded the Captain from the view of those on the quarterdeck, but he could clearly hear the conversation.

"Roast beef today, Ski."

"Yeah, I know, and we wear pea coats from now on."

"Whaddaya mean, pea coats?"

"Yeah, pea coats on the pier, Damn Exec says no more foul weather jackets."

"Well that ain't all, we got to polish this here brightwork 'til it shines every morning before quarters, Damn Exec says that too."

"Damn Exec."

Captain Speaks was shocked. "Why "Damn Exec" from these seamen?" he thought. It was easy to trace what had happened to the order the Captain gave the Executive Officer that morning. It was easy to see that the Executive Officer had passed it along in proper military manner. It was easy to see that the junior officers, leading petty officers, and lower petty officers were passing it along saying "The Exec wants ..." That's the way orders are passed along. Why? Because "it is easy."

"All ship's officers assemble in the wardroom," the boatswain's mate announced on the loud speaker system. Lieutenant Commander Lassiter escorted in the Captain. The junior officers took their seats when the Captain was seated. The Executive Officer remained standing. "Gentlemen, the Captain has a few words to say to us today."

The Captain rose and looked around slowly. "Gentlemen, we are continually exposed to words like administration, leadership, management, capabilities, organization, responsibilities, authority, discipline, and cooperation. You use these words every day. You give lectures to your men and use them, but if I were to ask you for a definition of any of these words I would get such a wide variety of answers that an expert couldn't tell what word we were defining. Some we probably couldn't define at all. We still use them, and will continue to use them as they are used in the continually mounting number of articles, instructions, and books we must read.

"If I were to ask any of you how we can improve leadership I would get answers filled with these words undefined and meaningless.

"If we listed all of the nicely worded theories of leadership, studied them, memorized them, and took a test in them, we wouldn't improve our ability as leaders one bit. I can tell a story, containing none of these meaningless words that will improve your leadership.

"In 1943, I was secondary battery officer in a cruiser in the South Pacific. In my second battle, gun control was hit and I lost communications with everyone except my 5-inch mounts. I could see that the after main battery turret was badly damaged and two enemy destroyers were closing us from at the time my 5-inch mounts were shooting at airplanes. I ordered to the two destroyers closing from astern. 'But Mr. Speaks, we're supposed to handle the air targets; who said to shift targets?' my mount captain asked.

"There was noise and smoke and explosions that day, but the explosion that I heard was not from a shell, but from those words of the mount captain.

"Those attacking destroyers got a few shots in at us before we beat them off. Maybe those shots found a target and some of my shipmates died. I never found out. There was too much other damage.

"I thought over the battle afterward and realized that this entire situation was my fault, not my mount captain's. I may have been responsible for the death of some of my shipmates because up to that day I always gave orders to my subordinates by attaching the originator's name to it.

"What does that mean? It means that it was the easy thing to do, to say, 'the gunnery officer wants us to shift targets.'

"In this peacetime world you may say that we no longer have this struggle on a life or death basis. Quick response does not mean life or death right now, but it might tomorrow or sometime after we've all been transferred elsewhere and this ship is being fought by people we don't know.

"Whether you're cleaning boilers, standing bridge watch or administering your training program, it's easy to say 'the exec wants' or 'Mr. Jones says.' It's the EASY, LAZY way; not the RIGHT way. You can sometimes discuss or even argue with an order, but when you give it to a subordinate, make him think it is coming from you.

"Giving orders the lazy way is like a drug. Once you start saying 'the ops officer wants' you will find yourself doing it more and more until you can't get a thing done any other way. Your men will pass along orders that way, too, and it will become a part of your organization right down to the lowest level. When some problem arises and you want action, you'll get 'who wants this' or 'why should we.'

"Each of you ask yourself if you have given an order today or yesterday in the lazy manner. I think almost all of us have. Now ask yourself if that order really originated with the person who gave it to you, or did they receive it from a higher level? We never really know, do we, but why should we even care?

"In almost every unit the 'lazy' ordering starts on a particular level. From personal experience I can tell you that this can be an exact measure of the unit effectiveness. If it starts at the department head level or higher it's a relatively bad outfit, and if it starts at the chiefs' level it's a relatively good outfit. You can find the level below which it starts by hearing a new title preceding a primary billet. 'Damn Exec' means that the executive officer is the lowest level giving orders properly. 'Damn division officer' means that the division officers are taking the responsibility for the order.

"Here I am using some of those words—responsibility and authority, those undefined terms we want to avoid, but perhaps we have helped define them.

"To be more specific, every officer does some 'lazy' ordering, but we need to do it less and less. We must try to push the 'damn' title down as far as it will go."

"Let's push the damn officer down all the way to the chiefs and below, then we will have a Damn Good Ship."

The story sums up what needed to be changed within the culture of ACU 4. You have probably heard the term "followership." It is the role held by certain individuals in an organization, team, or group--the capacity of an individual to actively follow a leader. Leadership and followership are like two sides of the same coin. Essentially everyone from the CO to the shop supervisor gives and receives orders. A leader must set the example when following orders as well as when giving them. Giving orders effectively is an art form. You must first ensure the order is necessary because inappropriate or unnecessary orders produce conflict, confusion, and ill will.

I started work on this issue over my first few weeks onboard, at which time I also met with the CO and debriefed my review.

CHAPTER 2

ACCEPT RESPONSIBILITY

U nfortunately, I deemed the fleet maintenance activity broken and unsustainable within just four months of my appointment. We needed to live up to our motto, "Above and Beyond," in maintenance and repairs by developing a self-sufficient organizational model. The fleet maintenance activity didn't have that stable platform to be able to back even 50 percent LCAC readiness. So when I say broken, I mean really broken. I had to take responsibility!

I informed the CO that I thought frustration made the sailors shortsighted. They identified so strongly with the command's apathetic culture that they were severed from the big picture. Even so, I needed them to look at things differently. I knew we must reorganize the structure of the maintenance department and fleet maintenance activity and increase the number of full-mission-capable LCAC by reinstituting a culture of accountability, documentation, and ownership.

"Let's plan this out and consider reorganizing the entire command's structure, not just the maintenance department and fleet maintenance activity," said the CO. "Please confer with Joe Green and Doug Keiler, both are retired captains, on the proposed model to ensure it aligns with the future maintenance requirements of the new ship-to-shore connector (SSC)."

When asked when I desired to take action, my reaction was a little on the extreme side. I responded, "Change this model, quickly!" I wanted to change things immediately because I realized what I had inherited was ineffective. "We can give it a few months to prepare everyone and start in November 2014, if ready."

"I concur," said the CO.

We eventually gave up on starting in November 2014 because it was such a short time to prepare. The CO had legitimate concerns about rushing and creating something that didn't have the foundation we envisioned and needed. It was a purposeful decision to continue planning and take the time to implement a strong foundation that would promote sustainability.

I considered improving LCAC readiness the primary goal at ACU 4 because it had been subpar for a while. Faced with mounting concerns over the effectiveness of the MD-FMA, previous leadership shifted emphasis to its pool of thirteen operating LCAC (known as Detachment Tango). Regardless, efforts were undermined by a reduction in manpower and resources due to budget constraints.

One key element I needed to ensure was the involvement o f LCAC community master chief petty officers (mid-level managers) in the LCAC training and maintenance rotation. An assigned LCAC community maintenance master chief would be responsible for the development of improved production processes and engineering methods, including shop layout and studies. I knew a seasoned LCAC community expert could perform the following crucial tasks:

a. Analyze workload and manpower requirements
b. Ensure a continuous screening program with team leaders was in effect
c. Monitor workloads and the performance of each shop and advise the maintenance control officer of current conditions
d. Evaluate best practices from lessons learned and watch out for potential replication opportunities
e. Ensure compliance with the planned maintenance system (PMS), related instructions, and publications

Figure 2.1 displays the maintenance department and fleet maintenance activity as an outlier from the notional mid-manager rotation. The master chiefs brought a wealth of knowledge and experience to the organization's operation and training departments. However, they bypassed the maintenance management positions in a seemingly strategic manner to avoid the most challenging leadership roles within the command. As a result, I often struggled to understand (and quantify) their true value and overall contribution to the LCAC program. I didn't wrestle with those thoughts very long. Earlier in my career, I learned not to try to fit my piece to someone else's puzzle— it's never a good look.

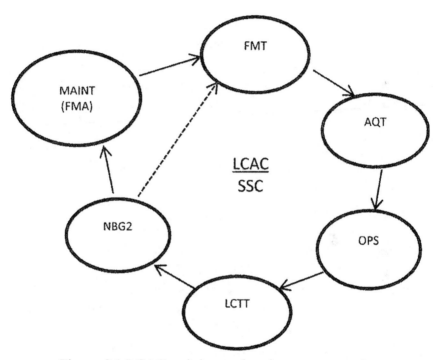

Figure 2.1 LCAC training and maintenance rotation

As we entered 2015, it was clear we were not ready to reorganize the command. "Let's continue preparations. It seems as though it's safer to start 1 April. Let's plan this out and give it six months and see where we are with it. We'll set goals and monitor progress," said the CO.

We needed to fundamentally change the way we operated as an organization supporting a fleet maintenance activity. We needed to move forward with a sense of urgency to implement necessary changes, but with no delusions of a silver bullet or quick-fix solution.

The navy way of life makes it imperative that the navy leader be willing and anxious to accept responsibility. This means I had to take the attitude expressed in these slang phrases: "Failure is not an option"; "I'm stuck like Chuck"; "I've got to see it through"; "I'm now on my own"; "I'm going to rise or fall with it."

This willingness to accept responsibility was difficult for me at first. Throughout my career, I have been consistently placed in environments where I was expected to take responsibility. ACU 4 was no different. I couldn't be "spoon fed" but had to assume full responsibility for developing myself into the leader who would make this epic reorganization work.

There are two common reasons why leaders are not willing to accept responsibility: laziness or the inability to plan. As a leader, I've had to develop both the ability to work and the ability to plan. Truly, every potential leader must be accustomed to hard work. Thus, I have learned that the more of a leader I become, the harder I have to work.

There is a mistaken notion that the higher one climbs in leadership, the more leisure time he will have. This is quite contrary to the actual situation. I've had to willingly accept the growing responsibilities placed on me, and throughout my time at ACU 4, I continued to manifest the ability to work long hours, work under pressure, and accomplish results in difficult conditions. My entire team was organized so that everyone got practice in hard work and was eventually able to demonstrate endurance.

The second requirement of the responsible leader is the ability to plan. This important ability requires careful and continuous development. The successful leader determines accurately the major goal he hopes to reach and sets up intermediate objectives, each of which puts him closer to his final goal. Establishing clear goals is the foundational part of planning. With goals in mind, the leader organizes resources and lays out a plan of action. In order to plan, the leader must possess broad knowledge, understand the facts of the general situation, and be able to exercise discriminating judgment. He must recognize the strengths and weaknesses of his personnel and appraise the material available to accomplish the given goal. I trained my managers to plan in each of these fields.

In February 2015, I didn't want to miss an opportunity for critical input and buy-in. I surveyed strengths apparent in my LCAC community managers' backgrounds and previous training. I used their strengths to point the way to future expectations that would make the reorganization successful. I involved leaders with a long LCAC maintenance and repair history as they would have the innovative perspectives needed. These leaders would know the fleet maintenance activity's uniqueness in the LCAC community, being the only East Coast-based LCAC maintenance facility.

We then had lectures, discussions, assigned reading, and analysis, which highlighted the nature and results of our planning. It was me and my small team of trusted advisers, but none more important than Senior Chief Petty Officers MacDonald and Chapman, who had enough confidence in the proposed reorganization model to break from party, putting their interest aside for the betterment of the LCAC program.

However, I had to push myself beyond appearance and provide practice in planning for given situations. Problems of planning, which involve the facts of a situation, had to be provided to my managers as frequently as possible. It was my role both to give them the chance to apply their prior knowledge and also help them acquire new skills necessary to plan our project quickly and effectively. It was critical for us to know where the organization was going—what was important, what was not, and what our goals were.

There were some managers outside of my trusted advisers who were willing to help me effectively implement the reorganization—even if they were secretly one of the culprits who contributed to the state I found things in. I had to do what I could to get them working with me and not against me. I wasn't looking for blind allegiance to the reorganization, but at least support in the effort.

So, there I stood before my trusted advisers, searching my mind for help and only found such aids as, "Be fair"; "Be tactful"; "Be military." That helped but little. I searched further and could merely recall that John Paul Jones said something in some fight and that Admiral Nelson spoke some inspiring last words. These things seemed vague and useless to me in the face of the real problem: leading change.

I then recalled the words of Robert F. Kennedy: "Progress is a nice word. But change is its motivator. And change has its enemies." I knew then that I had to take the lead in this problem and find ways to improve the effectiveness of my department and the fleet maintenance activity. I could not naively wait for someone else to take on this arduous task of reorganization. I was ready to make things happen myself.

I constantly kept my objectives in mind and resolved to act responsibly. I would be the leader the navy expected and wanted. The desire to be a leader is a matter of inspiration and of understanding. Several of my advisers had inspired the supervisors to want to be leaders, but I was informed that few had the understanding of what it truly meant to be a leader.

My goal was to inspire my advisers to be quality leaders, and I considered this to be one of my most important functions as we approached 1 April. This goal was not merely for the glamour and prestige of leadership; rather, I wanted to develop the men and women under me and to utilize my talents for the achievement of our plans.

In igniting their desire to grow in leadership, I had to make it clear to my advisers that our job was not an easy one. I emphasized the necessary hard work and the concerns that come with the responsibilities of leadership, which I personally carried with me every moment of the day and night. I wanted to be authentic and one of the hardest workers, all the while understanding I might get little credit for my efforts.

By mid-March, my adviser informed me the dissenters were few but vocal. Although we endeavored to include all stakeholders, there were those who refused to become part of the solution. Trash talking by those only interested in complaining, without offering any solution, had started. I soon realized I would be in for an enormous learning experience by heading the reorganization. If there was ever an opportunity to apply what I had learned up to this point as a leader, this was the time. What lay before me was the equivalent of a laboratory experiment, an attempt to formulate and test a more efficient and reliable maintenance protocol. I had to lead through this challenge using practical solutions.

In order to live up to our motto, "Above and Beyond," we made the necessary preparations to launch the reorganization on 1 April 2015. My team needed more than knowledge of the required manipulations and procedures. I had to instill in them a fighting spirit. I was not merely training my team to do a job—I was training them to do a fighting job. Without a fighting spirit, very few battles are won. My team must feel they were getting ready for battle, not merely trying to beat theirs or someone else's diagnostic or repair time. I needed them to realize that the sailor restoring a piece of vital equipment now may someday be doing the same in a hostile environment.

Attitudes are contagious. In teaching the fighting attitude, I had to possess it myself. If I exuded pride in the navy and demonstrated eagerness to take my place on the team, ready to fight and willing to battle because there is an important job to be done, my team would soon pick up something of my attitude.

Leading is both fighting and teaching. My advisers understood that those leading our teams must be more than those who direct operations or fight—they must also be teachers. Unless they taught our teams and trained our teams, the teams would not develop into efficient fighting units to carry out their commands under any conditions. Truly, leadership would be a crucial part of our reorganization plan, and I knew all my advisers must be part of this change.

CHAPTER 3

BUILD A SUCCESSFUL TEAM

On 1 April, we began ACU 4's reorganization. Leading a team effectively is the first rule of team building. The tough work of establishing my leadership with each team member was before me. I sought advice from my mentors on how to be an effective team leader. They all said the same thing: build relationships on trust and loyalty, rather than fear or positional power.

Teams don't come together by accident. Leaders must guide them through the three developmental stages: formation, enrichment, and sustainment.

Formation Stage

Teams work best when new members quickly feel a part of the team. The two critical steps of the formation stage are reception and orientation. A good sponsorship process literally made the difference between smooth and bumpy progression for new arrivals to my team.

Reception meant I extended my personal welcome to the MD-FMA, including a handshake and face-to-face greeting. The orientation stage began with meeting other team members, learning the layout of the workplace, learning the schedule, and generally getting to know the shops and environment. A sponsor was assigned to each new arrival to help him get oriented until he "knew the ropes."

The road ahead seemed long and hard. Across the command, six departments had begun to reorganize. In my area of responsibility, I now had up to 370 sailors, forty-nine mid-level managers, and twelve top-level assistant managers. We had several personnel mergers, which enabled me to have maximum personnel and provided sufficient

LCAC crew staffing, and it also compensated for the decrease in experienced/skilled personnel when cross-trained.

We had thirty-five LCAC to upkeep, with only 37 percent readiness. We needed structure to follow up on our strategy. My advisers and I developed our criteria by listing the problems we were trying to solve and the targeted opportunities that may exist. Then we prioritized each one. This became the criteria we used to evaluate the reorganization and to measure our success.

We discussed the broken processes and how various process improvements would work within the new structure. We also addressed the lack of procedural compliance and the inefficient duplication of efforts across the organization. My advisers clearly understood the most perfect structure could fail to meet our objectives if there was no change plan.

They informed me I needed to ask for the entire team's help in making the reorganization work. They thought that if the majority of the personnel assisted in creating the new organizational structure, they would then support it. And I added that those who didn't have an opportunity to help create it could be a part of its implementation. This enabled the best opportunity to receive valuable input and, thus, further tweak the structure.

Oh, I admit, we were challenged with the organizational change, but we also possessed the ability to bounce back with energy, effectiveness, and positive action. Over the next three weeks, my best principal adviser, Lieutenant Lashondra Phillips, headed maintenance control, the heart of LCAC maintenance. As the maintenance control officer, her thoroughness and keen foresight enabled the effective planning and scheduling of daily, weekly, and monthly workloads for the entire MD-FMA.

Maintenance Control was responsible for the coordination and scheduling of all craft maintenance, including restricted maintenance availabilities, Alteration Install Team, Post Service-Life Extension Program (SLEP) Extension, Fleet Modernization Plan, planned maintenance system, hourly maintenance packages, and countless hours of troubleshooting and repair. This complex operation is only made possible through the coordination between the maintenance control officer, leading chief petty officer, desk chief, team leaders, and work center supervisors. Critical to their success is direct coordination with all maintenance repair shop leads and daily face-to-face tasking and reporting of maintenance accomplishment. In a short time, Lieutenant Phillips established the necessary production foundation to ensure LCAC and all equipment were being maintained in a state of readiness, while ensuring priorities were being met.

My MD-FMA personnel were off to a great start. They embodied resilience as they identified and solved problems; gathered the right resources, people, and ideas; broke large tasks into defined and manageable steps; and found solutions. Yet, I still needed a knowledgeable LCAC community maintenance master chief more than ever. The individual filling the position would report to Lieutenant Phillips in the performance of assigned duties and would lead three (Red, White, or Blue) team leaders.

At the time, Lieutenant Phillips performed the responsibility of guiding these teams. My team leaders were responsible for the coordination and progression of all maintenance and production work on their assigned LCAC and served as the primary liaison between the twenty-two shops, desk chief (dispatcher), and Lieutenant Phillips. Phillips provided the outstanding management and foresight, but I needed someone with years of experience from the LCAC community to assist her in providing specific technical management of repairs and alterations. And then Lieutenant Phillips would be able to keep me advised of the overall workload and material situation as it affected the MD-FMA.

In figure 3.1, you will see how the MD-FMA was organized before reorganization. However, in figure 3.2, you will find the mergers and additions I spoke of earlier in this chapter.

MAINTENANCE DEPARTMENT-FLEET MAINTENANCE ACTIVITY
ORGANIZATION

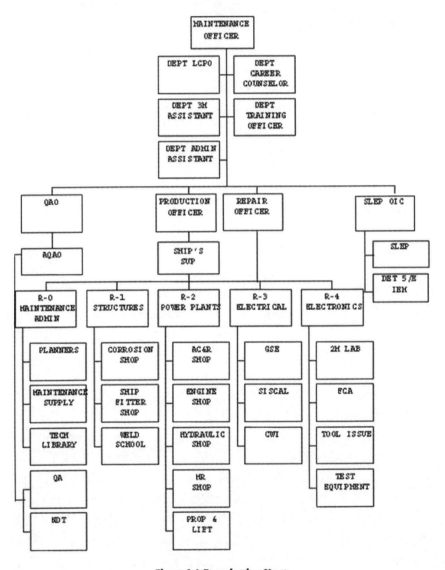

Figure 3.1 Organization Chart

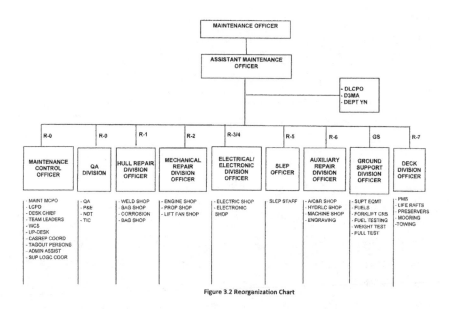

Figure 3.2 Reorganization Chart

One day while riding home in the late evening, I thought to myself, *Who is going to fill my shoes if I have to go on temporary assigned duty, take leave, or become sick?* I had to prepare my department for ongoing, smooth fleet maintenance activity in case of my absence. The reorganization was something that had never been done before. Therefore, I had to build a successful team that could do and be all that was required—with or without me.

On 1 May, four weeks after the start of the reorganization, my new assistant, Chief Warrant Officer 4 Gregory Collins, arrived. He was very knowledgeable on quality leadership and management. After reading his biography, I knew this seasoned engineering officer would fit well on my team. We had a lot of the same technical background. Now, I had someone who could fill my shoes if I was out of the office for an extended period of time. I just had to get him up to speed and on the same page to ensure the smooth performance of my department and fleet maintenance activity.

I remember working for people who ran their divisions or work centers from a notepad. I also can remember the chaos when I filled a gapped position—I couldn't do the same to ACU 4. Therefore, I thought back on the basic principles of planning and formed a contingency plan in the event of my absence. I knew Greg had a reasonable amount of time left at the command since he had just arrived. His leadership ability was readily apparent; he was being honored his first week at the command with a leadership award from his previous command. I was sure I had found the missing piece of the puzzle to continue the push toward becoming "Above and Beyond."

Within a month, Greg had the respect of both peers and subordinates, which was extremely important. After all, this is the person who would be in charge in my absence. He assisted me in obtaining the information for the forty-five-day reorganization survey. The survey was conducted to find out how the reorganization affected my MD-FMA team's quality of life and to obtain production metrics. The responses were so varied, it was a definite indicator that we needed the organizational change. We decided to continue to the six-month milestone.

In the meantime, I brought Greg into my confidence and demonstrated my approach to problems and decision making. When a decision had to be made, I discussed background information and requested his thoughts on the matter. Although not bound by his opinion, I quickly learned that I benefited from his vast experience, which often helped me to reach a different decision. This not only educated me, but also kept my leadership and managerial skills sharp.

At the end of each work day, Greg and I discussed advanced management principles until six or seven in the evening. I often used him as a sounding board for ideas; at times, he would play devil's advocate, trying to find holes in my logic and arguing both sides of our plans and decisions.

To accomplish the mission before me, strong leadership was essential. I had to take a page from the objective or goal of military leadership: "the creation and maintenance of an organization which will loyally and willingly accomplish any reasonable task, assigned or indicated, and will initiate suitable action in the absence of orders."

I now had pushed for organizational change, nearly tripled personnel accountability, was responsible for thirty-five LCAC, and had a team of advisers and a sharp assistant. The MD-FMA could only be as effective as its leaders, and I needed some of the best leadership to lead the twenty-two shops that were comprised of both sea and shore personnel.

One of my first actions in building a successful team was ensuring the right people were doing the right job. Without such coordination, capable people would not have been assigned the right tasks, and the MD-FMA would have been in a state of confusion. After discussing this with Greg, he said, "I have it for action." I knew it would be taken care of.

My second action was to hold the team together. We were a team organized to accomplish a mission that required the successful completion of a series of tasks. These tasks needed to be assigned and completed at a rate above the 37 percent readiness mark I observed when I assumed my position. Maintenance and repairs had to be inspected to ensure readiness, training schedules had to be prepared, and quality assurance standards had to be adhered to. Of course, it would be difficult for me to do all of these things alone, so this is where Lieutenant Phillips engaged the team leaders.

Enrichment Stage

I realized I had to gradually guide my new team and team members from questioning everything to trusting themselves, their peers, and their leaders. I hoped they would learn to trust by listening, following up on what they heard, establishing clear lines of authority, and setting high standards. The most important thing I could do as a leader to strengthen the team was training. Training enabled me to take a group of individuals and mold them into a team while preparing them to accomplish their missions. Training occurs during all three stages of team building but is particularly important during enrichment. It is at this point that the team is building collective proficiency.

I needed my team to bring a sense of professionalism to the job. Most had already undergone special preparation and training in the LCAC community, but there were some who had not. I needed everyone to possess the knowledge on which professional actions are based so that they could then conduct themselves in a polished and competent manner, to the ACU 4's advantage.

To ensure everyone was exhibiting professionalism, my officer advisers trained on developing these three attributes: technical competence, values, and ethical conduct. My team members needed to know their jobs and be able to do them well. Knowing their job and doing it well gave them an inner confidence, which, in turn, gave them a professional bearing. However, this confidence could also lead in the wrong direction, to an overbearing or "smart aleck" attitude, if they didn't develop their values along with their confidence.

Values include what is important to our lives, such as self-development, social values, or traditions we grew up with; economic values or what we would like to own; political values, such as loyalty to our country and the duty to vote; and religious values, like reverence for life and freedom of worship. All of these are related to the way we approach people. To develop professional values and attitudes, I simply resolved to let nothing be more important to me than the welfare of my team, the accomplishment of our mission, and our personal integrity.

My advisers held training discussions on personal integrity, which is based on our naval code of ethics, our sense of right or wrong. My advisers learned that their code of ethics is closely related to their values. Their values include what they wanted, but their ethics were more involved with the way they obtained what they wanted. Getting promoted may have been important to many of them, but they learned it was not ethical to advance by putting down other people through "back biting" and cheating. Additionally, they learned that if, on the other hand, they desired to improve themselves (value), they must work to improve their knowledge and ability (technical competence) and use methods that were fair and honest (ethical conduct). They were learning to be a professional team member.

Sustainment Stage

During this stage, members identify with "their team." They own it, have pride in it, and want the team to succeed. At this stage, team members will do what is necessary without being told. I needed my entire team to perform for the good of the other people on the team or crew—for the person on their right or left. It is a fundamental truth; sailors get the job done because they don't want to let their friends down. Similarly, the civilians with us felt like part of the installation and organizational team and wanted us all to be winners.

Every new mission gave us a chance to strengthen the bonds and challenge the team to reach for new heights of accomplishment. I developed my team because I knew they would be tomorrow's team leaders. It is important for any team to continuously train and maintain proficiency in the collective and individual tasks it must perform to accomplish its missions.

CHAPTER 4

WORK AS A TEAM

Our goal was to ensure ACU 4's success, which meant accomplishing the assigned mission. Through demonstration, motivation, and hard work, I needed my leaders to ensure all missions were accomplished. A leader's failure to ensure that his subordinates accomplished their task leads to the failure of ACU 4 to accomplish its mission and, thus, the failure of the military service in carrying out the larger mission. And if the military service fails, our country and way of life are in danger.

Within the military structure, there are two general areas of responsibility for every leader in every situation: (1) the responsibility to ensure the mission is accomplished and (2) the responsibility to support the subordinates who work to accomplish that mission. Completion of the mission is the first priority of leadership. How we accomplish the mission depends on the subordinates, the situation, and the leadership style.

In October 2015, we had reached the six-month reorganization milestone. I was building my team with a focus on teamwork, cohesion, and esprit de corps. Most of the concerns during the forty-five-day survey were starting to dissipate, and we were aligning ourselves to the new organizational maintenance philosophy.

I consider teamwork and cohesion to be measures of climate. I was looking for those team members who were willing to engage in teamwork and not selfishness. Selfless service is a requirement for effective teamwork, but to operate effectively, my twenty-two repair shops and the other departments needed to work together for our common task and mission objectives.

I encouraged my team to work together, while promoting group pride in accomplishments. Teamwork was based on commitment to the group, which, in turn, was built on trust. Trust means counting on team leaders and advisers to act for the team and keep its interests ahead of their own. However, I knew, at some point, I would have to do the hard work of dealing with breaches in trust, poor team coordination, and outright conflict. With this commitment in mind, we had to take special care in quickly integrating new members into the team.

Our goal was to encourage the team to be cohesive by setting and maintaining high standards. We understood that positive climate exists where good, consistent performance is the norm, but we were careful not to aim for a climate of perfectionism. Team members needed to feel that a concentrated, honest effort was appreciated, even when the results were incomplete. I wanted the team to feel that their leader recognized value in every effort as an opportunity to learn and get better.

My advisers recognized and explained to me that reasonable setbacks and failures would occur—whether the team did everything right or not. They expressed the importance of having a competent and motivated team, but informed me that weaknesses existed. I replied, "Let's ensure that our mistakes create more opportunities to learn something that may not have been previously brought to mind."

Sailors and navy civilians expect to be held to high but realistic standards. In the end, they feel better about themselves when they accomplish their tasks successfully. They gain confidence in leaders who help them achieve according to these standards and lose confidence in leaders who don't know the standards or who fail to demand quality performance. We weren't going to let them down.

If we were going to aim for "Above and Beyond," we had to have a sense of pride about us. Pride comes with success, but great teams do several things to build a sense of common purpose. It starts the moment someone new comes on the team. As we quickly integrated each new member, attention was paid to the way he was transferred in. That process was organized in advance and started before he even arrived, with a letter or packet sent ahead of time.

We expected great things from our sailors—to contribute and to do an excellent job, so teamwork was emphasized daily. People were encouraged to work together to accomplish the command's mission.

During the next several months, successes and achievements were recognized and played up to build a positive feeling about the command. Greg informed me that we needed to create more occasions for rewards and the recognition of accomplishments. We developed a Technician of the Month recognition program for junior personnel, E-5 and below. Since symbolic activities are used to build unity, we encouraged social activity and endeavored to make the work before us enjoyable.

When I asked one of my officers what he was doing to build positive attitudes, he replied, "I try to devote a small portion of the day to just being in the shop. I have tried to get to most of the sailors every day. When I'm in the shops, someone will say, 'Sir, I meant to ask you about this,' or 'Why are we doing this?' This affords me the interaction to ask, 'What do you think about this?' or 'What recommendations do you have about this?'"

His actions fed the morale and esprit de corps of his team. We had to be continuously aware of the mental states of our team members. Both personal and military problems affect the mental attitude of sailors, thus affecting the team's performance. Reorganizations are always disruptive, punctuated with challenges and risks. We did not take the task lightly. To help with the development of high morale, we followed the following guidelines, which improved our chance of achieving our objectives and minimizing disruption, unease, and cynicism:

1. Ensured basic needs were satisfied
2. Trained to the cause and mission
3. Instilled confidence in the team, their leaders, their training, and their equipment
4. Increased job satisfaction by carefully considering job assignments
5. Kept awareness of team concerns—the physical, moral, and spiritual welfare of team members, as well as that of their dependents
6. Established an effective awards program
7. Made members feel they were essential to the team
8. Recognized each team member's desire to retain individuality and to be treated as an individual
9. Encouraged the strengthening of ties to home, family, and religious groups
10. Maintained a professional atmosphere in training and administration

As we focused on building teamwork, cohesion, and esprit de corps, it quickly dawned on me that we were trying to build amid change. We had no choice but to face change. The MD-FMA's procedures, new organizational structure, and increased size made change especially daunting and stressful for some. Nonetheless, we had to be flexible enough to produce and respond to change by being proactive, not reactive. I charged my advisers to become a "future" group, charged with thinking about tomorrow.

My advisers thought one of the greatest challenges was in subordinates exercising initiative. Sailors and civilians not in leadership positions were often reluctant to recognize that a situation called for them to accept responsibility and step forward. Climate is largely determined by the degree to which initiative and input is encouraged. Leaders set the conditions for initiative by guiding members to think through problems for themselves, building confidence in their own ability to solve problems.

Building a successful team takes hard work, patience, and quite a bit of interpersonal skill, but it's a worthwhile investment. I learned that good teams get the job done. So, I would say, at the end of each meeting with any group of team members, "Let's get it!" This was my motivating chant to get my team to complete the mission on time with the resources given them and a minimum of wasted effort. There were six actions that enabled us to move forward as a team:

- Trusting each other and being able to predict what the other will do
- Working together to accomplish the mission
- Executing tasks thoroughly and quickly
- Meeting and exceeding the standard
- Thriving on demanding challenges
- Learning from our experiences and developing pride in our accomplishments

My team included many members who were not sailors. The contributions made by countless navy civilians and contractors are not forgotten. We acknowledge that many of our objectives could not have been achieved without the dedicated support of the navy's hard-working civilian team members.

As we progressed through the months, I learned that, despite all of our efforts, there was a small group of managers who refused to become part of the solution. I called them "disruptors" as they were vocal and bred discontent. Luckily, the core of my team embraced the reorganization and was growing accustomed to working together. They trusted one another and were accomplishing the mission, usually exceeding the standard without wasted effort.

Greg's development of a comprehensive Maintenance Department Organization and Regulations Manual (MDORM) could not have come at a better time. We sent it out to be vetted amongst managers and supervisors.

At nearly eight months into the reorganization, we assessed our progress. We found that there was a heavy reliance on Lieutenant Phillips' maintenance control personnel to schedule most repairs and clear up any conflict. For example, a water wash pump, which is designed to deliver water to the windshield of an LCAC, was inoperable. The gas turbine systems (electrical) technicians (GSE) diagnosed the water tank as being empty and could not continue. The line division (which I disbanded) pointed out that the GSE have deck mechanics and should be able to fill it themselves. However, the problem turned out to be a blown line, but it took two days of conflict resolution by maintenance control personnel to even get to that point. End result, it took three days to complete a very simple job and the LCAC missed several missions.

We also found that little thought was given to ensure the adequate number of personnel were available to fulfill assigned duties on both shifts. Most shops distributed their personnel by assigning the majority to day shifts and a small amount to night. We learned that keeping the majority of personnel on days worked well because a higher percentage of jobs were neglected and carried over to the night shift. Unnecessary situations were being created in not having enough personnel to perform operational tests of systems or being able to respond to casualties. Maintenance control personnel were frequently being used to augment the nightly shortfalls at the expense of their own duties. Fewer sailors desired to the work night shift because they knew they would have to work harder and expend longer hours than their day-shift teammates.

Communication was hard, but effective communication was harder. Very little information was being passed from shift to shift. At nearly every turnover meeting, a night shift sailor had no idea what was accomplished on day shift and vice versa. As a result, maintenance and repairs were reported as complete when they weren't, and troubleshooting efforts were duplicated.

Systems were being reported as repaired without being operational tested. For example, the Full Mission Trainer (FMT) team refused to accept an LCAC because there was no oil pressure indication on a gearbox. The GSE replaced the transducer and reported it repaired; however, the following day, the FMT team refused to accept the LCAC due to the same problem. It turns out that a broken wire, which was easily repaired, could have been identified if the smallest effort had been made to troubleshoot it and test it after the repair was completed. This situation resulted in two missions being missed, and it caused ACU 4 embarrassment.

Additionally, the disrupters desired to interrupt the progress we had made. They were less mature, and it took them some time to get up to the level of the rest of the team. Regardless of the meetings and checkpoints along the way to explain how things work and despite sincere attempts to make them feel like members of the team, they continued to cause issues. The disruptors had to learn the standards and the climate of the organization. I needed them to demonstrate acceptance and practice working together. I thought they could best oversee the integration process if they knew what to expect.

There are disruptors in practically every work environment, and to ACU4's disruptors, several of us were outsiders. We were considered outsiders because we were outside of the LCAC community, and, for some, until we became members of the community, we remained out. I learned that when non-LCAC community managers arrive, they are doubly set apart: not in the community and also an officer! Our years of experience as chief petty officers and engineers prior to commissioning are overlooked.

At the same time, the disruptors asked, "Who does he think he is? Just because he used to be a chief doesn't mean he has any authority over our community." We appeared to be outsiders because we had not gone through the LCAC training pipeline and would only be in the community for approximately two years—compared to their fifteen years or more. What could we know about the LCAC community? And we were assigned the job of leading and managing the LCAC mid-level managers.

I had received information that LCAC community Master Chief Brett Lee was due to arrive at ACU 4 soon. When he stopped by the command, I heard him speak with passion for the LCAC program. He had been in the LCAC community for more than fifteen years. We had a great conversation about the reorganization, and I knew he would be an asset to complete the team. He was a member of the in-group who could directly speak with the disruptors because he was the same rank as the highest ranking disruptors and senior to a few of the others. Again, the group of disruptors was small. However, once Master Chief Lee joined the team, I didn't find it difficult to become a bit closer to the in-group in relation to professional work. I don't mean on a "buddy-buddy" basis, but on a this-is-our-team basis. He was an LCAC community veteran who was motivated and eager to champion teamwork, esprit de corps, and communication.

The few disruptors who considered me as an outsider placed me in a delicate position because I had to lead them. I had to remember, and display, that I was there to help. On the other hand, I had the advantage that there was a natural tendency to look on me as a surface engineering expert—I arrived with this in my favor. I knew if I showed that I was the right leader, in time, the disruptors would soon understand and support my efforts. This didn't mean I was trying to win a popularity contest. It does mean that respect for the LCAC community, quality leadership, decorum, and common sense is always important.

I now had built a team that corrected the majority of issues that came our way. They provided continuous process improvement, quality maintenance, and procedural compliance. I had some of the best and most competent leaders, who were sensitive to the characteristics of the entire team and its individual members. Teams develop differently, and the boundaries between stages are not hard and fast. The great results they delivered determined what to expect of them and what was needed to improve their capabilities.

My team had excellent mental agility, or flexibility of mind. They were able to anticipate or adapt to uncertain or changing situations. Their agility helped them break from habitual thought patterns regarding the lack of procedural compliance, duplication of efforts, and poor cultural habits. They grew to improvise and quickly apply multiple perspectives when considering new approaches or solutions.

Thanks to a plethora of superior leaders and managers on the team, even the disruptors soon learned to reason critically while keeping an open mind to multiple possibilities. This allowed the team to reach a sensible solution and allowed each member to assist with organizational issues.

My team's ability to quickly isolate a problem and identify solutions allowed the use of initiative to adjust to change during daily operations. We had to instill agility and initiative within all of the team members by creating a climate that encouraged team participation. Identifying honest mistakes in the performance of their jobs made the team more likely to develop their own initiative.

The team began to use more critical thinking than in previous years. Critical thinking is a thought process that aims to find truth in situations where mere direct observation is insufficient, impossible, or impractical. It allows a more thorough thinking process and accelerates problem solving. Critical thinking implies examining a problem in-depth, from multiple points of view, and not settling for the first answer that comes to mind. In short, critical thinking is central to decision making

Critical thinking was our key to understanding the MD-FMA's changing situation. It helped us find causes and effects, arrive at justifiable conclusions, make good judgments, and learn from our reorganization experience. We needed this ability because many of the choices we faced required more than one solution. The first and most important step in finding an appropriate solution is to isolate the main problem. Sometimes determining the real problem presented an enormous obstacle; at other times, we had to sort through distracting multiple problems to get to the real issue.

However, we were able to resolve all of the problems found during our assessment. I think one of the main factors in our success was that our younger men and women had a strong, personal need for examples to live by, at least until they had formed their own principles. They expressed this need by following the example of some of my advisers and mid-level managers that they admired. They attempted to attach to and be like the leader they admired. As long as these sailors were not disillusioned with inferior leadership, ethics, values, and character, they continued to emulate their hero.

It was known amongst our team that we should hold such dignity and competence in all respects to inspire our younger sailors to emulate and respect us. I cannot overemphasize the value of setting a good personal example in your daily life. I informed my team leaders they could not live by the rule of "do as I say, not as I do" without the risk of subordinate team members regarding them with distrust or disgust, which would greatly diminish their reputation as a leader. Then again, outstanding conduct and leadership by my advisers, managers, and principle assistant managers could inspire others to follow the same pattern, thus benefitting the entire organization.

We could not expect others to support the reorganization if we ignored it. We knew we could not meet our mission (getting our LCAC to deliver a sixty-ton payload to a designated beachhead at speeds in excess of thirty-five knots) if we set an example of indifference. My advisers, managers, and principle assistant managers understood that rank has its privileges, but those privileges were not extended to cover deviations from the discipline of being a quality leader. We had to focus more on rank having its *responsibilities.*

The daily complaining had almost completely stopped as the few disruptors saw our positive results; LCAC readiness had increased from 37 percent to 65 percent. We identified various small areas needing change and changed them. I knew my team had something special, and we were growing in efficiency each day.

CHAPTER 5

PROVIDE QUALITY LEADERSHIP

Quality leadership is built on quality principles. Building on this solid foundation, leaders bring about change through influencing, motivating, and enabling others. Those under their command want to contribute to the effectiveness and success of their organization or team.

Quality leaders possess a multitude of common qualities. With this in mind, I wanted to channel all of my team's leadership efforts toward a shared goal. We didn't seek a new leadership formula to change the world. Instead, we sought to be smart and brilliant on the basics. We focused on the 10 Navy Leadership Traits and 11 Principles of Naval Leadership, which have been around for years, but some of the managers had not been exposed to the magnitude of their influence. There are actually fourteen leadership traits; however, we combined four within the ten remaining ones.

The leadership traits and principles were supported by a solid foundation: the Navy Leadership Competency Model. It is based on five core competencies, which can be applied to every level and position of leadership. I wanted to ensure we focused on competency because it is a learned behavior or set of behaviors that describes excellent performance in a particular work context (i.e., job role, position, or function). Superior performers achieve competency, resulting in better on-the-job results.
Leadership Traits

Leadership traits are the personality traits that lead to confidence and influence, while also promoting respect and loyal cooperation.

The ten leadership traits were the qualities of thought and action we wanted to demonstrate in our daily activities. These traits helped us earn the respect, confidence, and loyal cooperation of the entire team. It is very important that you understand the meaning of each leadership trait and how to develop it. Then you will know what goals to set as you work toward becoming a quality leader and a good follower.

Dependability means you can be relied upon to perform your duties and responsibilities properly. It means you can be trusted to complete a job. It is the willing and voluntary support of the policies and directions of the chain of command. Dependability also means consistently putting forth your best effort in an attempt to achieve the highest standards of performance. The MD-FMA team's dependability was increased by being where we were supposed to be on time, executing designed repair plans, not making excuses, and following through on every task to the best of our ability—regardless of whether we liked it or agreed with it.

Initiative is taking action, even though you haven't been given directions. It means meeting new and unexpected situations with rapid action. It includes using resourcefulness to get something done without the normal material or methods being available to you. We worked on staying mentally and physically alert. We were aware of things that needed to be done, and then we did them without having to be told. We aggressively sought out alternative, cost-effective repair options to forge craft readiness during a volatile fiscal environment— never deferring our organizational responsibilities or assigning lack of repair funding as a reason not to accomplish work.

Decisiveness means you are able to make good decisions without delay. You get all the facts and weigh them against each other. By acting calmly and quickly, you should arrive at a sound decision. You announce your decisions in a clear, firm, professional manner while being fair and consistent. A just person gives consideration to each side of a situation and bases rewards or punishments on merit. One must possess the ability to think about things clearly, calmly, and in an orderly fashion to make good decisions.

On occasion, we practiced being positive in our actions instead of acting half-heartedly or changing our mind on an issue. We didn't always get it right, but we continued practicing. We were honest with ourselves about why we made a particular decision, striving to avoid favoritism. We tried to be fair at all times and treat all things and people in an equal manner. And we avoided making rash decisions by approaching problems with a common-sense attitude.

Tact means you can deal with people in a manner that will maintain good relations and avoid problems. It means you are polite, calm, and firm. We teach people how to treat us through our actions. We tried to be courteous and professional at all times. We treated others with respect, as we desired to be treated.

Integrity means you are honest and truthful in what you say or do. You put honesty, sense of obligation, and sound moral principles above all else. We ensured the way we carried ourselves reflected alertness, competence, confidence, and control. We were honest and truthful at all times with one another as we stood up for what we believed to be right. We held ourselves to the highest possible standards of personal conduct. We tried never to be content with meeting only the minimum requirements.

Enthusiasm is defined as a sincere awareness and passion in the performance of your duties and responsibilities. If you are enthusiastic, you are optimistic, jovial, and willing to accept the challenges. We understood and believed in our mission to provide full mission capable (FMC) craft to the end user, which added to our enthusiasm for the work we had to accomplish. We even tried to understand the second and third order effects of why uninteresting jobs needed to be accomplished within a specific time frame. Our enthusiasm for consistently completing jobs on time resulted in repair efficiency and proficiency—leading to an all-time high of 72 percent LCAC readiness in as little as eight months.

Unselfishness means you avoid making yourself comfortable at the expense of others. Be considerate of others and give credit to those who deserve it. We avoided using our positions or ranks for personal gain or pleasure at the expensive of others. We were considerate of others, even during times when others weren't considerate of us.

Courage is what allows you to remain calm while recognizing fear. Moral courage means having the inner strength to stand up for what is right and to accept blame when something is your fault. Physical courage means you can continue to function effectively when there is physical danger present. We controlled the fear of change by practicing self-discipline and calmness in the moments of uncertainty. If we feared doing certain things that were required in our daily routine, we forced ourselves to do them until we had control of our reaction.

Knowledge is the understanding of a science or art. Knowledge means you have acquired information and understand people. Your knowledge should be broad, and in addition to knowing your job, you should know your organization's policies and keep up with current events. We increased our knowledge by remaining alert. We listened, observed, and researched things we didn't understand. We studied diagrams, technical manuals, and other military literature.

Loyalty means you are devoted to your country, the navy, and to your seniors, peers, and subordinates—unwavering loyalty up and down the chain of command. With this loyalty, you must possess the mental and physical stamina of endurance, which is measured by your ability to tolerate stress and adversity. We displayed our loyalty by never discussing the problems of the MD-FMA or ACU 4 with those outside, those who did not need to know. We never talked about seniors unfavorably in front of our team.

Once a decision was made and the direction was given to execute it, we carried out that mandate willingly, as if it were our own, reflecting the principle set forth in the "Damn Exec" article. For five days a week, we encouraged participation in physical training by modifying the daily start times. This enabled us to strengthen our bodies and finish every task to the best of our abilities by forcing ourselves to continue when we were physically tired and our minds were lethargic.

My team and I evaluated ourselves by using the above leadership traits to determine our strengths and weaknesses. These traits also proved to be extremely useful in determining our collective strengths and weaknesses. My team was encouraged to let go of garbage (bad practices) and take in quality traits to feel full. We began to have faith in one another and were no longer frustrated.

Leadership Principles

Leadership principles are the foundation of successful leadership and underpin the actions taken by the leader. These fundamental truths are developed through the consistent application of the leadership traits listed above. Work to improve your weaknesses and utilize your strengths. With a clearer understanding of yourself and your experience and knowledge of group behavior, you can determine the best way to deal with any given situation. You can improve yourself in many ways. For example, self-improvement can be achieved by reading and observing. Ask your friends and seniors for an honest evaluation of your leadership ability and utilize the eleven following leadership principles.

1. Know yourself and seek self-improvement.

Make an honest evaluation of yourself to determine your strong and weak personal qualities. You will have to seek the honest opinions of your friends or superiors to show you how to improve your leadership ability. Learn by studying the causes of success or failure of other leaders. Develop a genuine interest in people and have specific goals and definite plans to grow. Have a systematic personal reading program that emphasizes not only professional subjects but also includes topics to help you understand people, both as individuals and as they function within groups.

Members of my team made an honest evaluation of themselves to determine strong and weak personal qualities. We dedicated ourselves to overcoming the weak traits and further strengthened those areas in which we were strong. We sought the honest opinions of our friends or superiors to show us how to improve and studied the causes for the success or failure in other leaders, like Abraham Lincoln, Steve Jobs, and Napoleon Bonaparte. We developed a genuine interest in people and acquired an understanding of human nature. We mastered the art of effective writing and speaking. We had definite goals and definite plans to attain our goals.

2. Be technically and administratively proficient.

Before you can lead, you must be able to do the job. The first principle is to know your job. As a leader, you must demonstrate your ability to accomplish the mission; to do this, you must be capable of answering questions and demonstrating competence in your field. Respect is rewarded to the leader who displays competence. Administrative and technical competence can be learned from both books and on-the-job training.

My team knew what was expected and then expended time and energy to become proficient at those things. Early on, they formed a pattern of seeking to learn more than was necessary. I was not only impressed, but well pleased. They observed and studied the actions of capable leaders within the organization and engaged in meaningful conversation on what was learned. We spent time with those leaders who were recognized as technically and administratively proficient and learned as much as we could from them. We sought feedback from technically and administratively competent leaders concerning our own performance, and we were willing to change. Good leadership is best acquired through practice; therefore, each of us dedicated ourselves to preparing for the job at the next-highest rank.

3. Know your subordinates and look out for their welfare.

As one of the most important of the principles, you should know your team members and how they react to different situations because this knowledge can save lives. A sailor who is nervous and lacks self-confidence should never be put in a situation where an important, instant decision must be made. Knowledge of your sailors' personalities will enable you, as the leader, to decide how to best handle each person and determine when close supervision is needed.

We put the welfare of the women and men for whom we were accountable before our own welfare. We ensured grievances were corrected and discontent was removed. We ensured we were visible, which means we didn't sit behind the desk all day. I wanted our subordinates to know the leaders and feel we knew them. I knew we must be approachable.

We made the effort to get to know and understand the entire team. Someone from the team concerned himself each week with the living conditions of the members of our organization if they lived in the barracks. We ensured team members received the needed support from available personnel services. We tried to determine what our team's mental attitude was so that we could keep in touch with their thoughts. Sometimes we got it right, and sometimes we didn't.

We ensured fair and equal distribution of rewards, as well as created the Technician of the Month recognition program. We encouraged individual development and provided sufficient recreational time, insisting on participation. In many cases, we shared in the hardships of our sailors to better understand their reactions and to assist them in coping.

4. Keep your subordinates informed.

Sailors, by nature, are inquisitive. To promote efficiency and morale, a leader should inform the sailors in his organization of what is relevant and give reasons why things are to be done—when time and security permits. Informing them of the situation makes them feel they are a part of the team, not just a cog in the wheel. Informed sailors perform better and can carry on without your personal supervision if they are knowledgeable of the situation. The key to providing information is to be sure the sailors have enough information to do their job intelligently and to inspire their initiative, enthusiasm, loyalty, and convictions.

When necessary, my team explained why tasks had to be done and how we intended to do them. We asked the right questions to ensure team members were passing on necessary information. We were alert to detect the spread of rumors. Although we couldn't stop all rumors, we did replace most of them with the truth. In an effort to build morale and esprit de corps, we publicized information concerning the successes of the MD-FMA. Everyone on my team was informed about current legislation and regulations affecting their pay, promotion, and privileges through the MD-FMA newsletter, *The HoverCraft.*

5. Set the example.

As some members of the navy progress through the ranks by promotion, they all too often take on the attitude of "do as I say, not as I do." Nothing turns sailors off faster! It is the leader's responsibility to set the standards by personal example. Your appearance, attitude, physical fitness, and personal example are all on display by those in your organization. If your personal standards are high, then you can rightfully demand the same of those you lead. If your personal standards are low, you are setting a double standard and will rapidly lose their respect and confidence. Remember, your team reflects your image! Leadership is taught by example; it is the sum of those qualities of intellect, human understanding, and moral character that enables a person to inspire and influence a group of people successfully.

My managers displayed that they were willing to do the same things they asked the rest of the team to do. We had to be physically fit, well groomed, and properly dressed. We maintained an optimistic outlook and developed the will to win by capitalizing on the MD-FMA's abilities. The more difficult the situation, the better our chance to display an attitude of calmness and confidence.

We conducted ourselves so that our personal habits were not open to criticism. We exercised initiative and promoted the spirit of initiative on our team. We avoided showing favoritism to anyone on the team. By our performance, my team developed the internal belief that we were the best leaders for the positions we held. We effectively delegated authority and avoided micro-managing in order to develop leadership at all levels of the team.

6. Ensure the task is understood, supervised, and accomplished.

Before you can expect your team to perform, they first need to know what is expected of them. You must communicate your instructions in a clear, concise manner. Talk at a level your team is sure to understand, but not at a level that would insult their intelligence. Before they start a task, allow them a chance to ask questions or seek advice. Supervision is essential—without it, you can't know if the assigned task is being properly accomplished. Micro-managing is viewed by juniors as harassment and effectively stops their initiative. You must allow juniors to use their own techniques and then periodically check their progress.

On my team, we ensured an order was needed before issuing the order and used the established chain of command. We issued clear, concise, and positive orders. We encouraged the entire team to ask questions concerning any point in our instructions or directions they didn't understand. Their questions helped to determine if there was any doubt or misunderstanding in regard to the task to be accomplished. We then supervised the execution of our instructions, ensuring the team had the resources needed to accomplish the mission. Several of us varied our management or supervisory routine and the points which we emphasized during inspections. We exercised care and thought in supervision by not micro-managing because it damages initiative and creates resentment. On the other hand, a lack of supervision wouldn't get the job done either. Thus, we endeavored to provide the appropriate level of support.

7. Train your organization as a team.

Train and school, challenge and test, correct and encourage your team with perfection and teamwork as a goal. Discuss their roles and responsibilities; emphasize appropriate dress, bearing, and demeanor; promote self-improvement; and, most important, demand superior performance. No excuse can be made for the failure of leaders to train their team members to the highest state.

Train with a purpose and emphasize the essential element of teamwork. The sharing of hardships, possible dangers, and hard work strengthens an organization and reduces problems. Shared struggle develops teamwork, improves morale, and esprit as it molds a feeling of unbounded loyalty. And this comradery is the foundation for bravery, for advancing under difficult circumstances. Teams don't complain about training—they seek it and brag about it.

Teamwork is the key to successful operations and is essential, from the smallest division throughout the entire organization. As a leader, you must insist on teamwork while training, playing, and operating as a team. You must be sure each team member knows his position and responsibilities within the team framework. When team spirit is in evidence, the most difficult tasks become much easier to accomplish. Teamwork is a two-way street. Each member gives their best, and, in return, the team provides security, recognition, and a sense of accomplishment.

We ensured continuous studying and training, devoting specific times to provide focused training to our team in their particular areas of concentrations. Our goal was to maintain individual stability and organization integrity, while positioning our team for success in forthcoming positions of increased responsibility and authority. We cross-trained sea and shore sailors in the planning and executing of organization, intermediate, and depot-level repairs. We tried to keep in place as many of the team leaders as possible, if they were getting the job done, because needless transfers disrupt teamwork.

We emphasized use of the "buddy" system and encouraged participation in recreational and military events. We never publicly blamed individuals for the team's failure nor praised only one individual for the team's success. We ensured all training was meaningful and that its purpose was clear to all members of the MD-FMA. We acquainted our team with the capabilities and limitations of all other departments, thereby developing mutual trust and understanding. We based team training on realistic, current, and probable conditions.

Additionally, the CO had officially signed the MDORM. We provided forceful backup by insisting every sailor understood the roles and functions of the other members of the team and how the team functions as a part of the unit through review of the MDORM. Finally, we had a bipartisan document that delineated the key roles, duties, and responsibilities of the reorganization. We used it to train our organization as a team. It was sort of the icing on the cake to smooth out positions that did not have clarity, even before the reorganization. We decided that the MDORM would be updated at least annually to remain current.

8. Make sound and timely decisions.

As a leader, you must be able to promptly assess a situation and make a sound decision based on that estimation. Hesitation or reluctance in making a decision leads juniors to lose confidence in your abilities as a leader. A loss of confidence will create confusion and hesitation within the organization. Once you make a decision and discover it is the wrong one, don't hesitate to revise your decision. Your team will respect the leader who corrects mistakes immediately instead of trying to bluff through a poor decision.

My team developed logical and orderly thought processes by practicing objective estimates of the situation. When the time and situation permitted, we planned for every possible event that could reasonably be foreseen. We considered the advice and suggestions of our sailors whenever possible before making decisions and announced decisions in time to allow everyone, whether day or night shift, to make necessary plans. We encouraged everyone to estimate and make plans at the same time we did and to be familiar with our policies. I made sure my managers considered the second and third order of effects of our decisions on all members of the MD-FMA team.

9. Develop a sense of responsibility among your juniors.

To show the sailors on your team that you are interested in their welfare is to give them the opportunity for professional development. Assigning tasks and delegating the authority to accomplish tasks promotes mutual confidence and respect between the leader and juniors. It also encourages the subordinates to exercise initiative and to give wholehearted cooperation to the accomplishment of unit tasks. When you properly delegate authority, you demonstrate faith in your team and increase their desire for greater responsibilities. If you fail to delegate authority, you indicate a lack of leadership, and your subordinates may take it to be a lack of trust in their abilities.

We operated through the chain of command and provided clear, well-thought-out directions. We told the team what to do, but not how to do it. They were held responsible for results, although overall responsibility remained ours. We delegated enough authority to enable them to accomplish the task. At times, we were able to give our team members frequent opportunities to perform obligations usually performed by the next-highest level.

We were quick to recognize our team members' accomplishments when they demonstrated initiative and resourcefulness, while also correcting errors in judgment and initiative in a way that encouraged them to try harder. We avoided public criticism or blame, but we gave advice and assistance freely when requested. We let our team members know we would accept honest errors without punishment in return, and we taught from these mistakes by critique and constructive guidance.

We continued to resist the urge to micro-manage by not giving restrictive guidance, which destroys initiative, drive, innovation, and enthusiasm. Micro-management also would create boredom and increase the workload for leaders. We assigned our team members to positions in accordance with demonstrated or potential ability and were prompt and fair in backing our team, demonstrating our faith in them. We accepted responsibility willingly and insisted our entire team live by the same standard.

10. Employ your organization in accordance with its capabilities.

Successful completion of a task depends upon how well you know your organization's capabilities. If the task assigned is one that your organization hasn't been trained to do, failure is very likely to result. Failures lower morale and self-esteem. You wouldn't send an administrative specialist to perform maintenance on a piece of equipment, nor would you send three people to do the job of ten. Seek out challenging tasks for your organization, but be sure your organization is prepared for and has the ability to successfully complete the mission.

One of my top priorities was to ensure we were not volunteered for tasks we were not capable of completing. I didn't want the MD-FMA to fail or my team to think I was seeking personal glory. My advisers kept me informed as to the LCAC readiness and ensured tasks assigned to the team were reasonable. In an emergency, we didn't hesitate to demand their best. We analyzed all assigned tasks, and if the means at our disposal were inadequate, they informed me and requested the necessary support. We assigned tasks equally among the team and used the full capabilities of the MD-FMA before requesting outside assistance.

11. Seek responsibility and take responsibility for your actions.

You need to actively seek out challenging jobs for professional development. You have to use initiative and sound judgment when trying to accomplish jobs that aren't required by your position. Seeking responsibilities also means you take responsibility for your actions. You are responsible for all your organization does or fails to do. Regardless of the actions of your team members, the responsibility for decisions and their application falls on you. You must issue all instructions in your name and stick by your convictions. Do what you think is right, but accept justified and constructive criticism. Never remove or demote a team member for a failure that is the result of your own mistake.

I challenged my team to learn the responsibilities of their immediate senior and to be prepared to accept the fundamentals of those responsibilities should something happen. They sought different leadership positions that would give them experience in accepting responsibility in different fields. They seized every opportunity that offered increased responsibility. They performed every act, large or small, to the best of their ability. Their reward was increased opportunities to perform larger and more important tasks.

We stood up for what we thought was right and had the courage of our faiths. We carefully evaluated a team member's failure before taking action and ensured the apparent shortcomings weren't due to an error on our part. We considered the talents that were available, salvaged a member if possible, and replaced a member when necessary. In the absence of orders, my team was trained to take the initiative to perform the actions they believed their senior would direct them to perform if he was present.

The Navy Leadership Competency Model

The Navy Leadership Competency Model helps the leader take a group of people to a place they don't think they can go. It is based on five core competencies:

- Accomplishing Mission
- Leading People
- Leading Change
- Working with People
- Resource Stewardship

Accomplishing Mission

Accomplishing mission stresses accountability and continuous improvement, which includes the ability to make timely and effective decisions and then produce results through strategic planning, implementation, and evaluation. My team exhibited the skills of responsibility, accountability, authority, decisiveness/

risk management, continuous improvement, problem solving and technical credibility.

Leading People

Leading people is the ability to design and implement strategies that maximize personnel potential and foster high ethical standards in meeting the organization's vision, mission, and goals. My team exhibited the leadership skills of developing people, team building, crisis leadership, conflict management, leveraging diversity, and professionalism.

Leading Change

Leadership competency also involves leading change. This is the ability to lead your team toward the next level, to develop and implement an organizational vision that integrates program goals, priorities, values, and other factors. Inherent to it is the ability to balance change and continuity, creating a work environment that encourages creative thinking and innovation but is also a familiar and reliable environment. My team exhibited the skills of creativity and innovation, strategic thinking, external awareness, and flexibility. They also had the audacity and motivation to change the status quo after thirty plus years.

Working with People

Working with people involves the ability to explain, advocate, and express facts and ideas in a convincing manner. This leader can negotiate with individuals and groups internally and externally. My team exhibited the skills of influencing, negotiating, and partnering, both in oral communication and written communication.

Resource Stewardship

Stewardship is the ability to acquire and administer human, financial, material, and information resources in a manner that instills public trust and accomplishes the organization's mission. Now days, it also includes the use of new technology to enhance decision making. My team exhibited stewardship in their responsible financial management, savvy utilization of technology, and thoughtful management of the human resources available.

The Navy Leadership Traits, Principles of Naval Leadership, and the Navy Leadership Competency Model enabled the managers on my team to fully explore their potential. Although not new, it was the winning leadership formula for our reorganization and allowed us to be intelligent on the basics as we led our team to superior on-the-job results.

CHAPTER 6

"LET'S GET IT!"

L eadership builds effective organizations, and effectiveness is directly related to the core leader competency of getting results. My mantra was "Let's get it!" with the "it" being results. My leadership and management efforts were focused on accomplishing ACU 4's mission: "To provide combat-ready craft that fully meet operational tasking worldwide, on time, every time."

Mission accomplishment was a goal that coexisted with an extended perspective towards maintaining and building up the organization's maintenance capability for the future. Achieving began in the short term by setting objectives. However, achievement was based on the clear vision of getting results for the long term.

With my stellar group of mid-level managers overseeing the front-line supervisors and junior sailors, I was poised to integrate them with economic and technical resources to attain our goals. No matter what we attempted to accomplish, a thorough execution of management principles certainly increased our chances of meeting our goals.

We used professional management principles because it resulted in better performance, more clearly defined goals, higher success rates, and reduced waste. It made the difference between being materially postured for a successful operational deployment and being non-mission capable, unable to support the operational commander's required tasking.

Management is the business of developing and coordinating resources, both material and human, and directing their use effectively and efficiently to achieve a goal, objective, or mission. Although management is often described as both an art and a science, the formal study of management as a science is relatively new. The science of management can be learned in a classroom, but the art of applying this science in dealing with human beings must be learned through observation and experience. In our use of management, we achieved great results by skillfully blending study and application.

At ACU 4, we functioned at five general levels: executive management, top management, middle management, front-line management, and non-managerial. As listed above, my MD-FMA team operated along a continuum, from non-managerial positions to my assistant top-level manager, with me filling the top management level. Figure 6.1 indicates the typical navy management pyramid. The commanding officer and the executive officer are the executive level of management. Department heads are the top management level. Middle management is practiced at the division level. Work center or shop supervisors are front-line or first-level managers. Junior sailors (workers) make up the non-managerial level of the organization.

Whenever I said, "Let's get it!" I needed my team of managers to understand why their roles were so pivotal. We needed to group the types of management as either operational or administrative. At lower levels of management, we were mostly concerned with operational management. This involved motivating and directing front-line managers and workers to achieve our operational goals of getting the LCAC readiness to desired levels. My concerns often shifted toward administrative management activities that were commensurate with leading up to 370 people. My goals and objectives broadened in scope as my viewpoint of the organization's mission changed.

However, with few exceptions, my managers performed functions such as planning, organizing, staffing, leading, and guiding. My managers understood that those functions of management were interrelated, and if one of them was removed, getting results wouldn't occur.

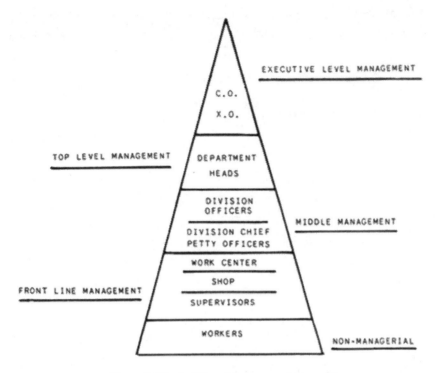

Figure 6.1 Typical Navy Management Pyramid

My managers spent a considerable amount of time balancing the needs and requirements of the twenty-two shops. We were responsible to the chain of command for attaining mission goals and objectives. However, we were also aware of and concerned for the needs of all of the sailors. Their health and welfare, desired advancement, career planning, and personal needs had to be considered. Collateral duties, human-relations programs, and equal opportunity requirements were evenly weighed. And we also had our own needs to worry about. Personal career planning, retirement planning, and family needs were aspects we had to coordinate with everything else.

Striking a balance between multiple conflicting needs as I kept mission objectives going made me feel overwhelmed at times. It was hard to remember some of the details when up to my hips in alligators. We adhered to the functions of management, which was a tremendous help in ensuring that we stayed on course. Without such guided focus, those alligators would have had me for lunch. While they are all individually important, the functions of management are also mutually dependent upon each other for success. The following is a brief explanation of these critical functions:

Planning started with setting a goal. Once this was done, the hard work started. Planning was the cornerstone of our management. All other functions hinged on careful planning. Without it, we were wasting our time and our organization's resources.

Organizing enabled us to arrange available resources in a coherent manner. This meant getting the needed materials and individual skill-sets to achieve our goal, setting up committees or work groups, and assigning authority and responsibility for various tasks.

Staffing was our process of selecting, training, and placing our team members where they were most effective. One of the lessons we learned was to consider the capabilities and temperament of our sailors when carrying out this function.

Leading involved motivating, disciplining, and directing our team members. Field Marshall Bernard Montgomery described leadership as "the capacity and will to rally men and women to a common purpose and the character which will inspire confidence." Our quality leadership was on display, and our example became more visible. Without strong, effective leadership within the chief petty officer's (CPO) mess, the best plans of getting results had a small chance of succeeding.

Controlling is the function that tied all the others together. We were able to develop the methods needed to monitor and guide performance. Without control, production efforts became disorganized and unsystematic. When controlling efforts drifted astray, we developed a plan to get things back on track and organized the means to carry out our original plan. Then, we assigned responsibility for getting production back on track through staffing—assigning tasks to personnel according to their strengths.

During the weekly LCAC status meeting, I directed my managers to use control methods to ensure production ran smoothly. Additionally, I desired that they use verbiage in their briefings that was associated more with leadership than followership. For example, during the meetings, one of my mid-level managers would say, "The starboard propeller is out of commission."

"What's wrong with it?" I asked.

"I'm not exactly sure. The shop is still troubleshooting. Hopefully, we will know something soon, but I don't think it's serious."

"When did this occur?"

"Probably yesterday or early this morning, sir."

I was thinking to myself, *Why am I just finding out about this? Why doesn't he know more? How can he, as a manager, develop a comprehensive repair plan and brief it with so many uncertainties?*

This type of followership verbiage needed to change. It was tough trying to change old habits, but I was able to get my managers on one sheet of music by instituting what I called MPIT. MPIT stands for "My plan is to…"

Within weeks, I could feel the empowerment in the room. For example, during the meeting, one of my mid-level managers would say, "Good afternoon, sir, LCAC 89's number eight lift fan bearing is out of commission as briefed to you earlier today. *My plan is* to place the craft in hangar bay number four today at 1430 and begin troubleshooting effort on night shift. I will brief you tomorrow morning on the root cause, estimated time of repair, and impact to mission readiness. This is the craft that will be used for Baltic Operations."

"Very well," was my only reply.

Therefore, by using the control methods and leadership verbiage, we were able constantly to repeat and reinforce the cycle of management functions. And I knew when my managers briefed the CO on the following day, we would bring great credit upon the MD-FMA team's efforts.

A major problem the armed services face today, during my tenure, is budget constraints. The budgets of our armed forces have not increased in a while. Although our system of doing business was adequate while working toward our LCAC goals, it didn't allow for many improvements in productivity. We also needed to procure new in-plant equipment. We had done an excellent job with the reorganization, but we needed to change in the way we did business.

We set our sights on a larger, system-wide objective to increase productivity through better quality maintenance and repairs. We focused the MD-FMA on the process by which work gets done. The group most familiar with that process was our sailors, the individual workers responsible for making it work. Several of our processes were either unmanageable or simply unworkable. My managers were responsible for making a particular job as easy as possible for workers. My supervisors and managers monitored the work process and responded to suggestions from the work force concerning unworkable procedures. Our sailors came up with nonstandard (but workable) solutions to problems. In some cases, it resulted in unsafe practices. However, these solutions were often extremely practical when executed with proper supervision.

We developed the ability to flush out these improvements and incorporate them into standard procedures, which served a dual purpose. First, it ensured the recommended improvement was usable and met all applicable standards. Second, the improved method was made available to everyone involved in that process. Both of these purposes served a practical application of "working smarter, not harder."

A popular myth among observers of the reorganization was that increased quality would result in increased costs and decreased productivity. Actually, improved quality ultimately resulted in decreased costs and increased productivity. When we focused on quality, it extended the time between failures on equipment and improved the efficiency of the operation of our fleet of LCAC. It reduced rework requirements and the need for waivers, departure from specification (DFS) or temporary standing orders (TSO). It also reduced mistakes and led to over $23.2 million in contractor cost avoidance to the US Navy.

Despite the typical barriers, some of the direct benefits were, as follows:

- Increased pride of workmanship among individual workers
- Increased LCAC readiness from 37 percent to as high as 72 percent
- Improved sustainability caused by extended time between equipment failures
- Greater mission survivability
- Better justification for budgets because of more efficient work
- Streamlined maintenance and production processes

We received "more bang for the buck" when we changed from management by results to management by process (quality) improvement. We didn't stop there. We continuously improved each and every process in the MD-FMA organization. That meant combining measureable methods, levels of knowledge, and professionalism to improve our internal processes. This cultural change in management practices had certain basic elements:

- Executive level management clearly stated ACU 4's mission. The CO stated the mission clearly and made it available to the entire organization. The mission statement prevented individuals from generating their own definitions of work priorities.
- My managers and supervisors ensured their actions clearly supported the organization's mission. This support included setting priorities and assigning tasks.
- As the MD-FMA leader, I had to focus our efforts toward a common goal. This focus was an important part of team building.
- Early on, I had to make a long-term commitment to quality improvement. My managers were tasked with setting an example by providing consistent, focused leadership.

We achieved results by focusing on the procedures and processes that got the work done. I made every effort to continuously improve work processes. The primary emphasis of this effort was the prevention of shoddy maintenance and repairs through quality improvement, rather than quality inspections. We had a Quality Assurance Division that could take care of that. Within the MD-FMA, we tried to manage quality from the beginning and conform to established specifications. As standards were met, we looked for new ways to improve maintenance and repairs. The most difficult part of my job was finding the means to further tighten standards and improve quality without adequate support from the executive and top-level management.

Another aspect of my focus was on the relationship between the MD-FMA as a customer of and supplier to the Supply Department. The MD-FMA and our Supply Department had dual roles. Our Supply Department established a working arrangement within ACU 4 that clearly defined each department's needs and realistic expectations. This mutual understanding of needs and capabilities was needed to achieve customer satisfaction. My managers made every possible effort to find out their customers' needs and to hear their customers' voices. They understood the importance of measuring and monitoring the degree to which their customers' needs were met or exceeded and continually endeavored to improve that.

I implemented policies and procedures and monitored the professional responsiveness of the MD-FMA, while encouraging my mid-level managers to maintain and strengthen our MD-FMA team. My mid-level managers anticipated and met the changing needs of the MD-FMA and customers. They monitored the performance of the twenty-two shops to ensure we were getting the desired results. They used metrics and team feedback to identify needs and ensure appropriate performance levels. And my front-line supervisors understood the importance of professional responsiveness and monitored the performance of individuals and maintenance teams to ensure work was done. The sailors responded professionally and competently to both internal and external demands.

My managers demonstrated the ability to plan, organize, and prioritize realistic tasks and responsibilities for themselves and their people. They used goals, milestones, and control mechanisms for maintenance projects. To achieve maximum results, they monitored and evaluated progress and outcomes produced by current processes, ensured continuous improvement through periodic assessment, and were committed to improving preventive and corrective maintenance to successfully accomplish goals.

Management and Process Improvement

I analyzed and defined complex policy issues clearly, in terms which permitted them to be dealt with in a practical way. I encouraged my advisers and managers to analyze, while I established broad performance expectations, focusing on results. I established effective management procedures and controls and also foresaw challenges to, and opportunities for, major maintenance availabilities, equipment upgrades, and installation. I continually reviewed the MD-FMA's reorganization for compliance with policies and procedures and to identify possible process improvements.

My mid-level managers isolated key points, central issues, and common themes to determine the best solutions or a range of options. They objectively analyzed the reorganization's strengths and weaknesses and took appropriate action. They monitored plans to accomplish work requirements, delegated appropriately, and ensured that effective internal controls were in place. They continually reviewed significant tasks and processes for possible improvement.

My front-line supervisors identified key information, central issues, and common themes to identify strengths and weaknesses of various approaches. They prepared work requirements and assisted their shops in preparing their work requirements. They planned, organized, and directed activities effectively to ensure that projects within their area of responsibility were completed in a timely manner.

My dedicated sailors planned and organized personal work activities, ensuring they contributed to successful performance of the MD-FMA team tasks. They looked for ways to improve personal performance and made recommendations up the chain of command to me concerning ways to improve work processes.

Decision Making and Problem Solving

To accomplish organizational goals, we identified and analyzed problems; used facts, input from others, and sound reasoning to reach conclusions; explored various alternative solutions; distinguished between relevant and irrelevant information; perceived the impact and implications of decisions; and committed to action, even in uncertain situations. We evaluated risk levels, created risk-control alternatives, and implemented risk controls. We were able to isolate high-importance issues, analyze pertinent information, involve civilians in decisions that affected them, generate promising solutions, and consistently render judgments with lasting, positive impact.

I made reasoned, effective, and timely decisions after considering all relevant factors and options. I implemented decisions and evaluated their impact and implications, making adjustments as needed.

My mid-level managers identified issues within the context of the MD-FMA, which required decisions or other action, and arrived at logical recommendations. They acted confidently and decisively within their own purview, relying on my guidance when needed.

My front-line supervisors carried out the decisions of my mid-level managers effectively and efficiently. They solved issues within their own authority and referred others promptly, providing all pertinent facts without bias.

My sailors solved routine problems and made appropriate decisions consistent with the performance of their primary duties. They kept their supervisor informed on matters requiring their involvement or supervision.

Conflict Management

We facilitated open communication on controversial issues affecting our micro-cultures (i.e. transgender; don't ask, don't tell (DADT) repeal, etc.) while maintaining professional relationships and teamwork. We effectively used collaboration as a way to manage contention. By confronting conflict positively and constructively, we minimized the impact to self, others, and the organization. We also reduced conflict and built relationships and teams by specifying clear goals, roles, and processes.

My mid-level managers, front-line supervisors, and I identified and took steps to prevent situations that could potentially result in unpleasant confrontations. We managed and resolved conflicts and disagreements in a positive and constructive manner to minimize negative impact.

Most of the time, my sailors resolved conflicts and disagreements in a positive and constructive manner to minimize negative impact. Sometimes the supervisors had to intervene.

Creativity and Innovation

We developed new insights into situations and applied innovative solutions to make improvements. We created a work environment that encouraged creative thinking and innovation by organizing think-tank and focus-group sessions to discuss complex issues and concerns. We took reasonable risks when deemed necessary and learned from the inevitable mistakes that accompany prudent risk-taking and applied this same thinking all the way down the chain of command. We encouraged innovation and helped the team apply the lessons learned. And we designed and implemented new or cutting-edge programs and processes, which we included in *The HoverCraft* newsletter.

I developed new insights into situations and applied innovative solutions to make organizational improvements. It was also important to me to foster a work environment that encouraged creative thinking and innovation.

My mid-level managers and front-line supervisors designed, recommended, and implemented new, cutting-edge programs and processes. They, too, encouraged creative thinking and innovation in subordinates. We always looked for ways to advance production through collaboration efforts.

My sailors applied innovative methods to accomplish individual and team tasks. They recommended innovations to their supervisors.

Vision Development and Implementation

We were able to envision a preferred future for the MD-FMA, setting this picture in the context of the ACU 4's overall vision, mission, strategy, and driving forces. Concerned with long-term success, I established and communicated organizational objectives and monitored progress toward objectives; initiated actions; and provided structure and systems to achieve our goals. We created a shared vision of the organization; promoted wide ownership; managed and championed organizational change; and engineered changes in processes and structure to improve organizational goal accomplishment. The reorganization was a success. And added to the excitement, we submitted a robust Secretary of Defense (SECDEF) Field-Level Maintenance Award package in January 2016.

My mid-level managers, front-line supervisors, and I influenced others to translate the shared vision into action. Together with the sailors, we used the shared vision to guide personal actions and to prioritize activities.

Effective management involved the use of planning, staffing, controlling, organizing, and leading. The essential component of our success was leadership involvement. We controlled the process that accomplished the mission. However, quality was in the hands of the sailors who did the job. This left us with the responsibility to drive out the natural fear of change and innovation that was part of most sailors' basic psychology. We were supported, from the CO all the way to the bottom of the chain of command.

In February 2016, ACU 4 celebrated its thirtieth anniversary. This served as a reminder that we operated and maintained the same LCAC that were first delivered to the fleet beginning in 1986. Despite the aging craft, the demand signal for LCAC operations continued to increase. The LCAC crews had flown 2,995 hours during 2016, the highest annual total flight hours in over eight years. With no additional manning or budget, the MD-FMA team answered the call by elevating readiness from 37 percent in 2014 up to as high as 72 percent in 2016, all because of innovation and smart maintenance practices.

1 April 2016, marked the one-year anniversary of the reorganization, commemorating a tremendous effort to boost readiness in support of amphibious operations. This was the direct result of the MD-FMA team's day-in and day-out dedication to mission accomplishment. I could not have been more proud. They continued to achieve this excellence by recognizing opportunities, understanding and eliminating true constraints, and by improving processes and maximizing available resources. The team had created an environment for success by developing specialists to manage their resources and improve their processes, focusing on the tenets of timeliness, quality, safety, and cost effectiveness. Through their efforts, the MD-FMA team executed 769,000 production hours and saved over $23.2 million in contractor cost avoidance for depot maintenance requirements for fiscal year 2016.

To get the results needed to go above and beyond, we structured what needed to be done so results were consistently produced. We embraced all actions to get the job done on time and to the standard by:

- *Providing direction, guidance, and clear priorities*, which involved guiding the team in what needed to be done and how.
- *Developing and executing plans for mission and task accomplishment*, which involved anticipating how to carry out what needed to be done, managing the resources used to get it done, and conducting the necessary actions.
- *Accomplishing missions consistently and ethically*, which involved monitoring organizational, group, and individual performance to identify strengths and correct weaknesses.

A critical element of getting results was adopting measures that supported a capability for consistent accomplishment. Achieving consistent results hinged on doing all the right things: having a clear vision, taking care of people, setting the right example, building up the organization, encouraging leader growth, and so on.

I am extremely proud of the dedication and accomplishments of the entire MD-FMA team and the impact they have had on our nation's ability to project combat capability. By empowering the workforce and creating a culture of continuous process improvement, they excelled at completing routine day-to-day maintenance, as well as complex, depot-level repairs and restricted availabilities (RAV) on time with zero production delays.

In May 2016, their efforts were further validated by winning the US Navy's nomination for the prestigious Secretary of Defense (SECDEF) Maintenance Award for fiscal year 2015.

The MD-FMA team's unparalleled accomplishments, dedication to continuous process improvement, and selfless dedication to the mission and its people enabled the highest readiness in nine years, although not ultimately winning the SECDEF Maintenance Award. Representing the navy as its nominee, for the first time in ACU 4's history, meant our accomplishments were earmarked as the best maintenance practices of any platform in the navy to sustain the highest level of material and combat-craft readiness to meet operational commander tasking.

Although I would say, "Let's get it," it was *my* primary responsibility to help the organization function effectively. ACU 4 had to accomplish the mission despite any surrounding chaos. This all begins with a well-thought-out plan, quality leadership, excellent management, and thorough preparation. We can now feel the pride and elation of living up to our motto: "Above and Beyond!"

CHAPTER 7

GO ABOVE AND BEYOND

Innovation describes our ability to introduce something new for the first time when needed or an opportunity exists. Being innovative includes creativity in the production of ideas that are original and worthwhile.

Sometimes a new problem presents itself or an old problem requires a new solution. You should seize such opportunities to think creatively and to innovate. The key concept for creative thinking is developing new ideas and ways to challenge your team with new approaches and ideas. It also involves devising new ways for the organization to accomplish tasks and missions. Creative thinking draws from previous similar circumstances or innovates by coming up with a completely new idea.

All leaders possess the skills to think creatively and adapt to new environments. Innovative leaders prevent complacency by finding new ways to challenge their team with forward-looking approaches and ideas. To be an innovator, you must learn to rely on intuition, experience, knowledge, and input from team members. Innovative leaders reinforce team building by making everybody responsible for, and stakeholders in, the innovation process.

Over the next year, my MD-FMA team continued to embrace an innovative mindset where each sailor applied their knowledge, skills, and abilities for their own success and that of the organization.

Along with innovation, one must generate the necessary energy to carry it through. One leader and manager who had innovation and the necessary energy was Charles Michael Schwab. He was an American steel entrepreneur. In 1880, an eighteen-year-old stagecoach driver gave up his job to become a clerk in a grocery store in Braddock,

Pennsylvania. He slept in the store and was at work from six in the morning until half-past ten every night. In his spare time during work, he would study mathematics.

Braddock was the location of the Edgar Thomson Steel Company's plant, and its steel workers provided the bulk of the customers for the store. A young grocery clerk took an enthusiastic interest in the big plant and began studying the development of the iron industry. Soon, he had decided there was more opportunity in steel than in groceries. One evening, the manager of the Edgar Thomson works, Captain Bill Jones, called the store to make a purchase; the ambitious clerk asked him for a job.

"Sure, I can give you a job," said Captain Bill. "You can start with driving stakes and carrying chains for the engineers. The pay is a dollar a day." As a result, Charles M. Schwab entered the steel business.

Driving stakes and carrying chains is exhausting work, but young Schwab leaped to the opportunity. He worked using all his energies during the day, and at night, he read several books on mechanics and engineering. He was preparing himself for more important tasks. Within six months, he was promoted to assistant engineer and then engineer. At the end of three years, he was in charge of the entire engineering corps.

Schwab, the ex-grocery clerk, had now become Captain Bill's principal assistant. He built eight gigantic blast furnaces at the Edgar Thomson plant, and the steel community throughout the country took notice. Then he designed and built the Homestead steel plant. When the plant was finished, Andrew Carnegie placed young Schwab in charge of it and made him a partner in the Carnegie organization. This was only seven years after leaving the town grocery store. He went above and beyond because of his amazing energy. This drive enabled him to become a steel manufacture technical expert, and he continued to grow his character traits in numerous areas, including leadership.

Mr. Carnegie recognized him as a leader and made him president of the Carnegie Steel Company. Schwab was selected as president of United States Steel Corporation when J. P. Morgan and his associates purchased the Carnegie and other steel companies and merged them to form the billion-dollar steel corporation. Schwab personifies energy. The phrase "human dynamo" has been misused in many cases, but it literally applies here.

Schwab was a dynamo—a producer of energy, a mighty generator of those powers of mind and spirit which drive men to hard work and enable them to thrive at challenging and unpleasant tasks in spite of disruptions or allurements. His great energy carried him over many insurmountable obstacles, empowered him to undertake big tasks, enabled him to tackle the most difficult problems, and made him ambitious for the highest achievement.

When he resigned from the presidency of the Steel Corporation, people said, "Schwab has made millions of dollars and resigned." The fact is that he was looking ahead to his biggest job and his greatest industrial achievement: Bethlehem Steel Corporation. He had acquired control of what was known as the graveyard of many fortunes because the plant had degenerated into a rusty clump of run-down machinery. Its business had fallen to its minimum, and there seemed to be nothing in the future except failure. Schwab, who was rich enough to retire and enjoy his wealth, decided to take on the arduous work of revitalizing and rebuilding the dying steel industry.

In 1916, he accomplished his goal, and Bethlehem Steel Corporation was one of the most noticcable steel producers in the world. It occupied more than thirteen hundred acres, encompassing busy rolling mills, shops, and furnaces. There were more than sixty thousand men employed, working its enormous plant day and night at the peak of capacity.

Schwab said to a writer of the *American Magazine*, "I always pity the man who says, 'When I get so much money, I am going to retire and enjoy life.' The greatest thrill that can come to any man is the thrill of successful accomplishment. In the last year I have had the opportunity to sell out Bethlehem for almost fabulous sums. They did not even interest me. If I gave up my business I would be resigning my greatest interest in life."

The secret of Charles M. Schwab's success was energy—resistless, moving energy. When he assumed control of Bethlehem Steel, he literally *owned it* and went to work taking it above and beyond. For three years, he punched the time clock as regularly and faithfully as the most routine worker in his plant. From seven in the morning to eight in the evening, he was on the job at the plant. He reorganized Bethlehem Steel and took them above and beyond.

Wherever Schwab went, he carried and communicated his admirable traits of character. His ambition was infectious, and his team worked hard, longing to take Bethlehem far beyond expectations. His team had confidence in him and he in them. His optimism and enthusiasm reinforced his confidence; his reliability proved it; and his energy demonstrated it.

The central trait in the character of Schwab that dominates and validates his entire being is energy—energy of body and mind! He went above and beyond because he was willing to work for it. High above the Hudson River, on Riverside Drive, stood his New York home. On the lawn was a large bronze figure of a puddler in an iron mill, a statue of hard work. Behind it were granite steps. The combination is significant because it represents a fitting symbol of the man who walked up the steps of experience and hard work from poor and humble beginnings to the home of wealth and power, which he had earned. His journey teaches us the importance of abstaining from the stress of what could have or should have happened—what has happened better prepares us for what's going to happen if we stay the course.

Schwab had been a hard worker all of his life. No man in his steel mills ever worked harder or more persistently than the owner himself. And from his work came the rewards, the natural fruits and inevitable results of energy wisely directed, rightly applied, and freely given.

And so it was in my case, and now it can be in yours. Energy is always the operational and winning quality. You may have ambition, confidence, loyalty, enthusiasm, and other character traits, but if you are without energy, you will remain a passive dreamer. The slowpoke is not the energetic type of leader. Energy is a dynamic quality. It's the character element which drives ahead; it acts. Energy utilizes confidence, loyalty, enthusiasm, and optimism and thrusts those who possess it forward to the achievement of ambition. It goes hand in hand with reliability because no leader can be reliable who is lazy and untrustworthy. Persistence, initiative, and self-control are each dependent upon energy. Yes, they are mere theory unless they are activated by the trait which stimulates productiveness and prompts a leader to work.

A strong work ethic and focused energy are within the repertoire of every leader. In contrast, it seems some people are born lazy, with inactivity and laziness instinctive to them. However, by the exercise of will power, habits of energy can be substituted for habits of laziness. There is no human nature so lethargic and lazily inclined that it cannot be recharged and revitalized under habits of purposeful work.

One of the strong controlling factors in the development of energy as a character trait is *health*. If you place yourself in a condition of physical fitness, you will immediately find your energy quickening. Good health is a prerequisite to the development of normal energy. Therefore, to cultivate energy, pursue health through right habits of exercise, eating, working, and leisure. Without proper alignment among these habits, it is nearly impossible to keep your energies up to the peak efficiency.

In my twenty-two years of naval service, I have seen the energetic leader, manager, and supervisor communicate this trait to others just as surely as the enthusiastic leader, manager and supervisor communicates enthusiasm. A hard worker will frequently have a more stimulating effect upon a lazy associate than countless words of threat or discipline. And the opposite is true as well; a hard worker surrounded by procrastinators is likely to fall into lazy habits. It is only by exercise of willpower that he can keep himself strong against the influence of idle associates.

Therefore, your second aid to the cultivation of energy is *environment*. Seek to synergize with those who are alert, eager, and genuinely active in perfecting their craft. Whether in military service or business, you may be exposed to lazy and procrastinating workers, but your willpower can minimize their influence. You can keep yourself to your normal energy by looking ahead to your goal, keeping alive all your interest in your work, and selecting only people who are of like energy as your close associates.

The traits of ambition, confidence, enthusiasm, optimism, and reliability are powerful stimulants of this energy. All pleasant feelings tend to develop energy. If you are truly ambitious, you must be a person of energy or else your ambition will weaken and falter. If you have confidence, you are eager to go ahead and act. Enthusiasm and optimism feed energy and incentivize your efforts. It's important that your initiative and persistence have the cooperation of energy, or your desire to be successful will be no more than a desire or an inclination.

Your third aid to the cultivation of energy is the *development of the other character traits*. Round out your character in the other basics, and you will find your impulse to act and achieve becomes stronger and more powerful. Your energy will grow with your character development.

Your fourth and most important aid is *willpower*. In fact, willpower is the necessary catalyst to each of the preceding aids. Without willpower, you cannot control your health; without willpower, you cannot affect your environment; without willpower, you cannot control the other character traits. Without willpower, you cannot make energy a controlling habit of your life.

With willpower, however, you can work miracles in the development of your character. Willpower can carry you over a bad start. It can neutralize a wrong environment, and it can substitute good habits for bad habits.

Willpower will overcome the negative effects of being overcautious, too calculating, or fearing failure. It will substitute a positive, assertive attitude for the attitude of "don't care." It will develop interest in working hard and relieve the deadening influence of work. It will make you strong to turn away from all influences that diminish energy, and it will give you power to establish energy as a consistent habit of action.

Laziness may seem to be an inherited quality, but willpower can overcome laziness. Energy may seem to be a gift bestowed upon a few favored individuals, but willpower can develop it in any man. You can develop work power within you. And hard-work power is the power that achieves, the power that accomplishes results to go above and beyond.

In April 2017, I closed the doors to my position as the leader of MD-FMA team, though not before submitting the 2016 SECDEF Maintenance Award package. I turned over what was my most difficult job to date. I reflected for a moment, recollecting the nearly three years I had given voice to the organization's motto, "Above and Beyond," throughout the command. It sounded great, but the model was broken, and the organization was far from living up to its motto. Well, I would give some credence if *above* referred to LCAC operating inches above the surface and *beyond* described their ability to carry out assault missions on foreign beaches beyond the horizon. Nonetheless, my innermost goal was to work hard and generate enough energy so that by the time I departed, we would be enthusiastically living, thinking, working, and speaking "Above and Beyond"—just like our sacred motto.

As a leader, I did my job. I selected my team members carefully so that they fit the duty and the duty fitted them. I organized the work in such a way that every person knew what to do, had enough to do, and knew where he was going and where he was. I did my absolute best to motivate my team in such a way that their energy and morale were soaring high. I captured my sailors hard at work by posting pictures throughout the command to showcase their unique talents. I expanded the repair capabilities by procuring state-of-the-art industrial plant equipment (IPE) to include computer numerical control (CNC) machining, 3-D printing, advanced hydraulic testing, and 2M module test and repair capabilities.

The IPE upgrades undoubtedly helped to reduce many arduous tasks for the MD-FMA. However, none provided more return on investment (ROI) than the addition of various office and shop comforts. The addition of new desks, chairs, flat screen televisions, printers, tricycles (yep, bikes), quality tools, and decorative signage with our motto, "Above and Beyond." My team then had a sense of swagger, walking with an increased sense of ownership and confidence. And that was good for me to see, my friend!

Using an established and proven approach to quality repairs, my MD-FMA team managed to operate with the efficiency of a Fortune 500 company while embracing the reduction in manpower and resources subsequent to manning shortfalls and budget constraints. My

MD-FMA team achieved excellence by recognizing opportunities, understanding and eliminating true constraints, improving processes, and maximizing available resources. Most noteworthy was the authorship and directing of the epic reorganization of ACU 4's maintenance philosophy as we realigned manpower and resources encompassing six hundred sailors on sea and shore duty.

Our efforts were further validated by the high level of materiel and combat readiness by which we deployed LCAC—demonstrating the innate ability to meet the operational commander's tasking repeatedly. When these phenomenal men and women elevated LCAC readiness from 37 percent to as high as 72 percent, it was the highest that had been recorded in ten years. This amazing feat increased efficiency through implementation of innovations and repair strategies, intrusive leadership, and improved quality assurance procedures and processes across various disciplines. Throughout my three-year term, our team's unwavering determination, steadfast devotion, and dedication to maintenance excellence has exceeded all professional and performance expectations.

These accomplishments were not achieved alone but with the support of the remaining ACU 4 departments not heavily impacted by the reorganization. They provided unprecedented technical support, inventory control, and material management for twelve deployed LCAC between fiscal years 2014 and 2016. They recorded a myriad of outstanding achievements while participating in several multinational exercises and maintaining mission-ready LCAC to train for future encounters.

I led my team in achieving the desired goal of living up to our motto in such a way that the MD-FMA organization is better and their morale is higher than when we embarked on the reorganization. They went *above* the average and are positioned to go *beyond* expectations.

We achieved all we set out to achieve, and every issue I deemed detrimental to our success at the beginning is no longer an issue. We started newly assigned personnel off right by a sponsor program, including an explanation of the organization's history, traditions, and present role. We developed the feeling that the organization must excel and go above and beyond. We recognized and publicized achievements of the organization and its members in social media and publications. We made use of ceremonies, symbols, and slogans. We used completion to develop teamwork and made proper use of decorations and awards.

To my surprise, I was nominated and selected as winner of the 2016 Claud A. Jones Award (Fleet Engineer of the Year) by the American Society of Naval Engineers (ASNE). This award is given to a fleet or field engineer who has made significant contributions to improving operational engineering or material readiness in our maritime forces during the past three years.

I learned during this journey that to be an effective leader, you must know your professional strengths and weaknesses. The Marine Corps has a written leader's code, which I used as a guideline to make an honest evaluation of my team and my own leadership. We were able to improve our weak areas and exploit our strong areas. The Leader's Code is, as follows:

> I become a leader by what I do. I know my strengths and my weaknesses and I strive constantly for self-improvement. I live by a moral code with which I set an example that others can emulate. I know my job and I carry out the spirit as well as the letter of orders I receive. I take the initiative and seek responsibilities, and I face situations with boldness and confidence. I estimate the situations and make my own decisions as to the best course of action. No matter what the requirements, I stay with the job until

the job is done; no matter what the results, I assume full responsibilities. I train my men [and women] as a team and lead them with tact, with enthusiasm, and with justice. I command their confidence and their loyalty: they know that I would not assign to them any duty that I myself would not perform. I see that they understand their orders, and I follow through energetically to ensure that their duties are fully discharged. I keep my men [and women] informed and I make their welfare one of my prime concerns. These things I do selflessly in fulfillment of the obligations of leadership and for the achievement of the group goal.

In self-evaluation, we read each sentence of the leader's code and asked ourselves, "Is this what I do?" If our answer was no, we became aware of an area of personal weakness and considered how it should be improved. Granted, it was not used to make or break us as leaders but to simply guide us in the progress of our self-development.

CHAPTER 8

SUCCESS IS YOURS

Although my job of leading the MD-FMA at ACU 4 is over, the wisdom, skills, and abilities of the journey have stayed with me. I want to keep the energy going by encouraging you to go above and beyond, starting with where you currently are. Learn to make firm decisions; without the power of decision, you are useless as a leader. When a person presents a problem to you, that person expects a clear-cut decision. Discuss complicated questions or those clearly beyond your authority to decide with an immediate superior; resolve the lesser issues decisively yourself. Never allow the fear of making a mistake or looking ridiculous deter you from attempting to solve a problem.

You will make mistakes occasionally, but an honest mistake seldom involves ridicule or criticism if all fundamentals of the problem were appropriately considered. From mistakes come experience and growth and from experience and growth comes wisdom. With experience, growth, and wisdom, success is yours for the taking.

You are your own manager, managing the knowledge, skills, and abilities within you. Are you on the job? No one else can possibly see your faults, comprehend the mysteries of your mind, supersede your ability to picture your own great ideals and purposes, dictate the policies and events of your own life, or efficiently get work and results from your skills and abilities. Who's running your organization, anyway? You are the manager. Again, are you on the job?

Most of us are just assistant managers, allowing someone else to do our thinking for us. We want the impressive titles and credit—but avoid doing the work. If you are not on the job, I recommend you call a meeting of your own intellectual capabilities. Close and lock the door; then get down to business. Take your seat at the head of the table to discuss candidly and without restrictions the real things that concern your success. Keep in mind: you are the leader in charge, the actual manager who can take yourself above and beyond.

Throughout this story, you have learned to be a fighter, not with fists or weapons, but through the principled mastering of your skills and abilities. Great victories are won from the everyday battles of life over the endless difficulties that will almost hourly face you. Therefore, fight facing forward—ferociously, yet fairly. When everybody looks down on you and calls you a loser, that's your signal to finish the fight and win.

Today, what is your work? Make it personal and gather the best that's in you and succeed. Go out to meet and overcome every obstacle that seeks to keep this day from being the one you will most value. Don't give up any territory, fighting every inch of the way. Go to bed with the satisfaction of a conqueror who goes above and beyond expectations.

I think to work hard is to be ethical, whether we use machinery or a pen. Don't be the one manager who dishonors his organization by being afraid of the job—no matter how demanding or difficult it may be. You cannot be in fear of someone else above you, behind you, or alongside of you.

You must possess a sense of independence and be yourself. The results will take care of themselves. Honor your organization, and it will honor you. Be positive and pursue your work with energy and the belief that you know your work. In time, you'll find that others realize you are doing that which moves the organization above and beyond.

There will be those managers who think to avoid hard work is the easiest thing to do. However, it is always easier to face hard work. The most expensive lessons are many times learned late in life. The managers who avoid hard work have caused timidity and fearfulness to set in when facing problems. Many of them evaded a problem earlier in their career that could easily have been solved at that time. But they refused to work hard or deal with problems until they were compelled to face them later. It takes greater courage to decide to work hard than it does to actually work hard.

You should work hard today and face the challenges ahead of you. If there has been more important work given to you than you are doing now, face the new work and decide to master it. Whatever may be standing in your way, face it with courage and without fear. Don't sidestep or avoid anything. Face it and finish it, closing the loop.

Gather together the energy of hard work and experience and use them as a rope with which to pull yourself higher. When you are moving up, you must assist the one who is down. When you do your best, you are conscious of a satisfaction that the very act itself produces. The word "excuse" must not be in your dictionary if you are to be willing and determined.

Have you ever used an excuse as a prop? Excuses hinder you and form stumbling blocks, causing your fall unless you kick them aside. Excuses are abnormal and wear false faces. They never seem as they really are. And excuses never answer anything. The next time you feel like making an excuse, don't! You are either on the sidelines or in the game.

If you are on the sidelines, you are simply watching. You are inactive and contributing to your personal pleasure. If you are in the game, you are working hard; you are getting pleasure in rendering service. You will always get more pleasure out of the game if you are a player instead of a spectator.

All over the world, there are organizations with spectators. The hard workers are the ones who compensate for the inadequacies of the spectators. Don't allow someone else to do what you should be doing yourself. To merely hold a job title doesn't count for much. You have to *be* the job in every aspect, or the perception may be that you are the spectator, contributing neither to self nor the organization.

As a spectator, you will miss out on true pleasure, growth, and increased power. If this is you, break the habit. When a task comes before you, take hold of it and do it. You have to be the one who is quick to respond to any call from the organization at the moment someone else evades. Work that you should do is never done better when shifted to someone else. This is a personal matter of success or failure.

Which will you be, the spectator or the doer? The spectators are easily spotted because they perform most of the easy jobs in organization. They are the managers that are too busy to do what is asked and required of them. Only those who feel an unconscious consciousness lurking within them, informing them they must not stray too far, can maneuver back to the game.

When you are working hard, you have several alternatives if one of your efforts fails—or succeeds. Try to learn two moves at once: the move you intend to make and the one you see in your mind ahead of that one. For example, a supervisor envisions himself in the job of assistant manager (the move he intends to make) and is not satisfied until he reaches the roles of manager (the move he saw in his mind ahead of assistant manager). Everybody seems to admire and look up to the manager of resources, just as everyone looks up to the leader who makes the move to be an expert within the organization.

Rainy days come to us all, no matter how smart we may be. Even so, you must continue with all of your energy to move forward. In doing so, be reminded there is sure to be an element always ready to condemn and find fault with every forward act. You are sure to be judged, primarily by the manner in which you take criticism. The greater you become in independence and willpower, the more fierce and determined will be your critics and fault-finders.

Don't judge me or my performance at ACU 4 by my critics. Judge me by the way my MD-FMA team now receive me. Among them, you will find an appreciation of my motive, which is the key to unquestionable and honest criticism. Every thought you think either builds up or tears down. Your positive thoughts build; your negative thoughts tear down.

Do not fear any task before you. If you happened to walk into an undesirable situation as I did, don't fear it. Most organizations have their problems—small ones, large ones, funny ones, peculiar ones, and secretive ones. But you can't be afraid, and no harm can possibly come to you so long as you feel confident and unafraid. Therefore, work through it. Work through fear, problems, and criticism and deal with spectators head on. Do not worry your way through a situation or waste time complaining. Real managers, leaders, innovators, go-getters, and doers work through it all.

It's not as easy as it seems because you may have to go through brick walls that look absolutely impossible and impassable. However, the way to get through them is to work through them. Hard work is a soother, strengthener, and key ingredient of success. When you are in doubt as to your next best move within your organization, while newer things are up-and-coming around you and while so many managers are doing their best to make their offices a better place, you must work through what has been handed to you and to do it in a way that makes the organization a better place than it was before you arrived there. In doing so, you will realize there are always better things ahead.

You will not find much benefit in standing still and complaining. There is always some good in making an effort toward something beneficial to the organization. Even if others oppose or laugh at you, go ahead and do the hard task. Forward motion and a resolute spirit is the secret of inspiration.

Inspiration isn't what comes *to* you but what comes *out* of you. There are so many managers waiting for inspiration. They tell themselves that when it comes, they are going to rebuild the organization. However, you'll see these managers at their lowest possible potential throughout a long career. They take no steps forward but will criticize the work of those who have gone ahead of them. You often find such managers waiting for their inspiration—indefinitely.

You can't wait. You must get things done through the inspiration within you. Essential to this endeavor is perseverance and personal fortitude. You have to plan on working hard and then do it. Observe how inspiration oozes through your every step. After all, you do want to go above and beyond—don't you? If so, partner with inspiration. If you do something for inspiration, it will do something for you. And you don't have to be perfect to get its attention.

It is an inspiring thing to meet a manager who has never learned to evade issues. If an unpleasant situation arises within the organization, the easy and lazy thing to do is to get out of it the best way possible. But the only sensible way is to face the situation. It is energizing to face your issues because they may not be half as difficult as you first imagine. Every problem looks difficult at the start, but the minute you decide to take it on, it diminishes about half.

This optimistic way of thinking keeps you moving in the right direction. You need to strive to be an optimist because it enables you to walk in the sunshine, rather than in the dark. You will enjoy happiness and discover less failure as an optimist because everybody is always anxious to associate with an optimist, to invite him to lunch and to have him around for conversation.

Being an optimist is one of the most profitable assets in an organization—not from the standpoint of dollar value only, but from the viewpoint of soul value. Optimism helps when you are trying to do a tough job with all of your ability, working hard and exerting energy. Optimistic energy reduces your work and enhances your abilities; your infectious positive outlook and cheerful energy leads, lifts, and inspires others on the team. To live in a world of energy is to live in a world of affection, brilliance, achievement, and service power. Like a magnet, the power of energy is able to bring promising things and like-minded people your way.

Energy perseveres, organizes, reorganizes, and strategizes—each day, each hour, and each minute. Energy is a power, a living thing within you that will never go away if commanded under your willpower to stay. This enables the people on your team to be influenced by your hopeful presence.

Just as soon as your energy leads you to think or do something worthwhile for the organization, you begin to have influence. Influence is something that has no boundaries. It makes you a part of someone else. Remember, your influence is never entirely absorbed nor does it disappear; it counts repeatedly and has no end.

The three greatest objects in life—friends, happiness, success—are each dependent on proper influence. So it is good to know that you can send it out to scatter brightness or darkness. It's your choice. One of your greatest responsibilities as a manager and leader lies in the way you acquire and give out your influence.

The influence you have on your team is sure to have a remarkable bearing on the total work of the organization. Your influence on others and their influence on you are sure to become a force and a factor in the entire body of work supporting your organization's mission. If you keep your influence spot-on and nourishing, it will go out and return that same way to you.

As you influence others, you must remember to give credit and appreciation to them if they are performing to standards. Don't keep anyone from that which gives life to his confidence by leading him away from hope. Give credit where credit is due. This is an important step for you and your team's ability to go above and beyond. When you keep giving credit, more honor and credit comes back to you, so magnanimously applaud those on your team. If asked who on my MD-FMA team most deserves the credit for our success, I happily respond, "There is enough credit for us all!"

I am proud of my trailblazing MD-FMA team. They paid a heavy penalty, but the price has been cashed and redeemed into inspiration. The entire ACU 4 team is now able to say we provided the best quality training to our people; maintained all LCAC and equipment in the highest state of readiness through economical, timely, and high-quality craftsmanship; and provided the best possible administrative, financial, logistical, operational, and technical support.

While leading the MD-FMA team of professionals in service and achievement wasn't easy, it was worth it. The work, the sweat, the hardships, the misunderstanding of the reorganization, and the loss of associates even—which forwardness of vision seems to always demand—count as little to me as I have witnessed my team succeed. I was not afraid, and I have to admit, I like the appearance ahead of us better than the appearance that is behind us.

I learned that to lead is to inspire and develop others to lead. Successful organizations owe a lot to their leaders—those who made the path—and also to those who dug in and made improvements and innovations.

No matter how menial you think your task may seem, if you keep your eyes forward and work hard, you will be part of the leadership of the present, which forms and molds the future. If you feel what you do, there will be greater things accomplished in your organization.

Whatever you say, whatever you do, ensure you feel it. And if you can't feel it, then don't say it, don't do it.

During the first Great War, the United States Government decided to build a city of warehouses on the flat, marshy waste bordering on Newark, New Jersey. Large storehouses were necessary to accommodate the supplies to be shipped to France.

One of America's leading engineers was consulted and said that it was absolutely impossible to carry out the plan. Three months later, the same engineer and builder stood at the same location and saw done what he truly believed couldn't be done.

Edward H. Harriman was told he could not build the railroad across Salt Lake City, Utah. "All right," he said, "go ahead and do it!" He went above and beyond.

William G. McAdoo built the tunnels underneath the Hudson River in New York after dozens of attempts had failed. Many laughed at him when he said he intended to go ahead and do it. They don't laugh now, for he did it.

Almost anything can be done with ideas, plus the willpower and hard work to see them through. It's strange how the sooner you get started at doing what seems to be the impossible, the more convinced you'll become that the thing is completely possible.

You can make yourself invaluable within your organization through hard work. You can increase your energies until they become works of power. You can dream and make your dreams become achievements. Achievement is an impression in your mind, and you should never allow the impression to fade away. The inspiring thing is to be a creator of impressions and bring them all to fruition. You are the only person who is able to always interfere with your success and achievements. There is no power in existence able to change your direction, slow you down, or take your faith and determination.

One impression I would like for you to place in your mind is that of a ladder. It always points up, and there is something of a lesson, a metaphor, in the ladder. It always begins at the bottom and constantly has room at the top. You can choose the ladder you most desire, one with a dozen or a thousand rungs. The longer the ladder, the higher you will be when you reach the top.

Abraham Lincoln decided he wanted a ladder with many rungs. As a result, he went from that miniature Kentucky log cabin to the presidency of our nation. As you climb the ladder, don't forget that the strength you accumulate at the lower rungs will increase with every rung you climb higher. You must go rung by rung, not trying to skip one or two. In skipping, you will slip or fall practically every time—forced to begin all over again.

Pick a long ladder to slowly climb it. Don't be concerned about the naysaying, disruptive crowd below—keep your eyes on the rung at the top, and you will go above and beyond.

Today, I implore you to work hard because *today* is what you have. It's also what you are and what you do. Yesterday is not an issue—it has past. Tomorrow is no problem—it isn't here. However, today is here and so is opportunity. History depends on today. Take hold of your chances to spread your good traits of ambition, confidence, enthusiasm, optimism, and reliability within your organization. Today is the day, your day.

Today is time and change doing its job, so don't fear it. For all concerns and things that don't count, let them go because this day will never come again. You are capable of doing great things, so take the initial plunge and clear any barriers to your success. The water is never as cold as it may appear to be. You've read my story and know that I have already taken the plunge. I am pleased to inform you to, "Come on in; the water's just fine!"

Your success within your organization is going to be measured by your promptness to recognize the things you should do and your ability to immediately do them. Your measure of success in your career is going to be judged in the same way, in everything that comes up to you for decision. Keep in mind the initial decision takes the most courage.

Take the plunge and decide today that you will work hard and use all the greatness within you to do what is necessary to go above and beyond. Days, weeks, months, and perhaps years from now you can look down from the ladder and realize your choices, decisions, and actions have enabled you to go above and beyond.

Success is yours. I'll see you at the top!

AFTERWORD

Leading and managing organizational change is not an easy task. I want to encourage you through one of my favorite quotes. It's from the speech "Citizenship in a Republic," delivered at the Sorbonne, in Paris, France, on 23 April, 1910, by Theodore Roosevelt. It is affectionately known as *The Man in the Arena*:

> It is not the critic who counts; not the man who points out how the strong man stumbles, or where the doer of deeds could have done them better. The credit belongs to the man who is actually in the arena, whose face is marred by dust and sweat and blood; who strives valiantly; who errs, who comes short again and again, because there is no effort without error and shortcoming; but who does actually strive to do the deeds; who knows great enthusiasms, the great devotions; who spends himself in a worthy cause; who at the best knows in the end the triumph of high achievement, and who at the worst, if he fails, at least fails while daring greatly, so that his place shall never be with those cold and timid souls who neither know victory nor defeat.

You must realize that being a leader and manager of change is not about giving orders; rather, it's about earning respect, leading by example, creating a positive climate, maximizing resources, inspiring others, and building teams to promote excellence. Along the way, you will make honest mistakes and face difficult decisions or dilemmas. This is all part of the process of learning the art of leadership and management. You must internalize the best values, demonstrate unimpeachable integrity and character, and remain truthful in what you say and do. Then, you will be trusted as a leader and manager. You must never break that trust because it is the core of leading and managing change.

GLOSSARY

Assault Craft Unit FOUR (ACU 4) is a navy amphibious command located at the Joint Expeditionary Base Little Creek in Norfolk, VA.

Advanced Qualification Training (AQT): Advanced training for LCAC crew personnel.

Brightwork is exposed metal on a naval ship, usually brass or bronze that is kept polished rather than painted.

Commanding Officer (CO) is the officer in command of a military unit.

Chief Petty Officer (CPO) is the seventh enlisted rate (E-7) in the United States Navy, just above petty officer first class and below senior chief petty officer (E-8).

Deck force (or deck department) comprises sailors who perform a variety of functions depending on ship type and size. Examples include maintenance and upkeep of the ship, handling of the ship's rigging and ground tackle, coordination of underway replenishment operations, conductance of minesweeping operations, maintenance and operation of the ship's boats, supervision of diving and salvage operations (including towing), and serving as shipboard seamanship specialists. Undesignated seamen, or those who have not selected a rating (e.g. job or vocation), are normally the most junior sailors on board and are usually sent to the Deck Department for their first assignment.

Destroyer (DD) is a fast, maneuverable long-endurance United States Navy Ship warship built after 1921 intended to escort larger vessels in a fleet, convoy or battle group and defend them against smaller powerful short-range attackers.

Departure From Specification (DFS) is a lack of compliance with an authoritative document, plan, procedure, or instruction.

Disruptor is a person who interrupts or impedes progress through confusion or disorder.

Executive Officer (XO) is the second-in-command of a military unit, reporting to the commanding officer.

Fleet Modernization Plan (FMP) is the navy's primary means for updating LCAC's communications and operating systems.

Fourteen Thirty Hours (1430) is Military Time using 24-hour clock notation, which is 02:30 PM using 12-hour clock notation.

Full Mission Trainer (FMT) is LCAC simulated training in an amphibious environment and dynamic responses together with actual LCAC systems operation.

Gas Turbine Systems Technician (Electrical) (GSE) is a navy rating in which sailors operate, repair and perform organizational and intermediate maintenance on electrical components of gas turbine engines, main propulsion machinery, auxiliary equipment, propulsion control systems, and assigned electrical and electronic circuitry up to the printed circuit and alarm warning circuitry.

Industrial Plant Equipment (IPE) such as lathes, hydraulic machines, welding, machining equipment, etc., maintained using the Navy's planned maintenance system.

Joint Fleet Maintenance Manual (JFMM) is a single, unified source of maintenance requirements made up of five distinct volumes. This manual serves as a standardized, basic set of minimum requirements to be used by all Type Commanders and subordinate commands; clear, concise technical instructions to ensure maintenance is planned, executed, completed and documented within all Fleet commands; and as a vehicle for implementing Regional Maintenance policies across all platforms.

Landing Craft Air Cushion (LCAC) is a high-speed, over-the-beach, fully amphibious landing craft capable of carrying a 60-75 ton payload. It is an air-cushion vehicle (hovercraft) used by the United States Navy's Assault Craft Units.

Lieutenant Commander (LCDR) is a mid-ranking officer rank in the United States Navy, with the pay grade of O-4.

Landing Craft Air Cushion Training Team (LCTT) is responsible for developing a well-trained LCAC crew capable of operating the craft in arduous environments.

Amphibious transport dock, also called a landing platform/dock (LPD) is an amphibious warfare ship, a warship that embarks, transports, and lands elements of a landing force for expeditionary warfare missions.

Lieutenant (LT) is a United States Navy commissioned officer rank/grade O-3.

Master Chief Petty Officer (Master Chief) is the ninth, and highest, enlisted rate (E-9) in the United States Navy, just above senior chief petty officer and below senior chief petty officer (E-8).

Maintenance Department-Fleet Maintenance Activity (MD-FMA) is responsible for the overall maintenance and repair of ACU 4's fleet of LCAC.

Maintenance Department Organization and Regulation Manual (MDORM) provides comprehensive guidance for the safe and effective operation of the Maintenance Department.

Naval Beach Group TWO (NBG2) is Commander, Naval Beach Group TWO, an Immediate Superior In Command (ISIC) staff that supports four subordinate commands that provide 100% of the amphibious connector support to the Atlantic Amphibious

Fleet: Assault Craft Unit FOUR (ACU 4), Assault Craft Unit TWO, Amphibious Construction Battalion TWO (ACB-2), and Beachmasters Unit TWO (BMU-2).

Operations Officer (OPS) is the officer who leads the operations department. He understands the global environment where the navy operates as well as the organizational context of how navy missions are defined and assigned.

Outsider is a person who does not belong to a particular group.

Planned Maintenance System (PMS) is maintenance management system designed to maintain equipment within specifications through preventive maintenance, identifying and correcting potential problems before the equipment or system becomes inoperable.

Post Service-Life Extension Program (SLEP) is to extend the LCAC's service life for another decade, increasing its life expectancy to 30 years by sustaining and enhancing craft capability, replacing obsolete electronics, repairing corrosion damage, increasing survivability and establishing a common configuration baseline.

Quarterdeck is the stern area of an upper deck or part of a deck on a naval vessel set aside by the captain for ceremonial and official use.

Restricted Availabilities (RAV) is when an LCAC goes through regular periods of maintenance, repairs and upgrades.

Safe Engineering and Operations Program (SEAOPS) provides a system to standardize operational procedures, training and training scheduling for LCAC.

Secretary of Defense (SECDEF) is the leader and chief executive officer of the Department of Defense, an Executive Department of the Government of the United States of America. The Secretary of Defense's power over the United States military is second only to that of the President. Secretary of Defense Maintenance Awards Program recognizes outstanding achievements by field-level units engaged in military equipment and weapon system maintenance within the Department of Defense. Six Secretary of Defense Maintenance Awards are presented units from small, medium, and large categories.

Senior Chief Petty Officer (Senior Chief) is the eighth enlisted rate (E-8) in the United States Navy, just above chief petty officer and below master chief petty officer (E-9).

Ship-to-Shore Connector (SSC) is a system proposed by the navy as a replacement for the Landing Craft Air Cushion (LCAC).

Temporary Standing Order (TSO) is a written discourse that authorizes action with the authority of the commanding officer and provides specific guidance for a period of time for critical situations.

WEB log is a database used to improve the LCAC hourly package tracking.

REFERENCES

Adams, George M., *You Can,* 3rd ed., Frederick A. Stokes Company, New York, 1913.

Coast Guard Leadership Competencies, Commandant Instruction M5351.3, *Leadership Development Framework*, United States Coast Guard, Washington, D.C., 2006

Fundamentals of Marine Corps Leadership, Marine Corps Institute 033N, May 1999.

Generating Energy, (Charles M. Schwab) Article, adapted from *Course in Business Essentials*, Volume 4, by Business Training Corporation, pages 73-82, 1916.

Management Fundamentals a Guide for Senior and Master Chief Petty Officers, NAVEDTRA 10049, Naval Education and Training Manual, Training Command 0502-LP-2 12-8600 (TRAMAN), 1990.

Megginson, Leon C., Donald C. Mosley, and Paul H. Pietri, Jr., *Management: Concepts and Applications,* 3rd ed., Harper & Row, New York, 1989.

NAVPERS 16154: *Manual For Practical Development Of Leadership Qualities,* 1944.

Navy Leader Development Program, Chief Petty Officer Student Guide, NAVEDTRA 38222, Chief of Naval Technical Program, Memphis, Tenn., 1990.

Quote from *Citizenship in a Republic* Speech (also known as *The Man in the Arena)*, delivered by Theodore Roosevelt at the Sorbonne, in Paris, France on 23 April, 1910.

Standard Organization and Regulations of the U.S. Navy, OPNAVINST 3120.32B, Office of the Chief of Naval Operations, Washing- ton, D.C., 1986.

Total Quality Management, Department of the Navy, Washington, D.C., 1989.

USAF Managers' Course, Vol. 3, *Leadership and Management, Course 12,* 00012-03-8112.

USAF Extension Course Institute, Gunter Air Force Station, Montgomery, Ala., n.d.

U.S. Navy Regulations,1990, Office of the Secretary of the Navy, Washington, D.C., 1990.

Washbush, John B., and Barbara J. Sherlock, *To Get the Job Done,* 2d ed., Naval Institute Press, Annapolis, Md., 1981.

Also by Dennis L. Richardson

Naval Engineering
Principles and Theory of Gas Turbine Engines

ISBN-13: 978-1524648572
ISBN-10: 1524648574

Naval Engineering: Principles and Theory of Gas Turbine Engines is a technical publication for professional engineers to assist in understanding the history and development of gas turbine engines including the thermodynamic processes known as the Brayton cycle. Common principles of various gas turbine nomenclatures, technical designs, applications, and performance conditions that affect the capabilities and limitations of marine operations are provided. It enables the ability to describe the principal components of gas turbines and their construction.

This book will enable the reader to increase professional knowledge through the understanding of navy engineering principles and theory of gas turbine engines. The reader will learn the operation and maintenance of the gas turbine modules (GTMs), gas turbine generators (GTGs), reduction gears, and associated equipment such as pumps, valves, oil purifiers, heat exchangers, shafts, and shaft bearings. Inside this book, you will find technical information such as electronic control circuitry, interfaces such as signal conditioners, control consoles, and designated electrical equipment associated with shipboard propulsion and electrical power–generating plants. When every detail of engineering work is performed with integrity and reliability, technical leadership know-how will improve.

Made in the USA
San Bernardino, CA
14 December 2017